Queen Victoria

Very Interesting People

VIP

Bite-sized biographies of Britain's most fascinating historical figures

Queen
Victoria

Very Interesting People

K. D. Reynolds and
H. C. G. Matthew

OXFORD
UNIVERSITY PRESS

Great Clarendon Street, Oxford ox2 6DP

Oxford University Press is a department of the University of Oxford.
It furthers the University's objective of excellence in research, scholarship,
and education by publishing worldwide in

Oxford New York

Auckland Cape Town Dar es Salaam Hong Kong Karachi
Kuala Lumpur Madrid Melbourne Mexico City Nairobi
New Delhi Shanghai Taipei Toronto

With offices in

Argentina Austria Brazil Chile Czech Republic France Greece
Guatemala Hungary Italy Japan Poland Portugal Singapore
South Korea Switzerland Thailand Turkey Ukraine Vietnam

Oxford is a registered trade mark of Oxford University Press
in the UK and in certain other countries

Published in the United States
by Oxford University Press Inc., New York

First published in the *Oxford Dictionary of National Biography* 2004
This paperback edition first published 2007

British Library Cataloguing in Publication Data

Data available

Library of Congress Cataloging in Publication Data

Data available

Typeset by SPI Publisher Services, Pondicherry, India
Printed in Great Britain
on acid-free paper by
Clays Ltd, St Ives plc

ISBN 978-0-19-921758-8

10 9 8 7 6 5 4 3 2 1

Contents

Preface

As founding editor of the *Oxford Dictionary of National Biography* (from which this life of Victoria derives), Colin Matthew decided early on to write the accounts of the modern monarchs himself; in so doing he followed the practice of his predecessors on the first, Victorian edition of the *Dictionary of National Biography*. Knowing the scale of the task and the extent of his other commitments, from the beginning he asked me (a former graduate student of his, and one of his team of in-house academic editors at the *Oxford DNB*) to co-author the biography. We drew up a plan and divided the work.

Colin's expertise was obviously to be directed towards the political aspects of Victoria's later career, my own to the earlier period and the details of court and family life. We had very different views of Victoria. Colin was inevitably influenced by his long editorship of the *Gladstone Diaries*, and his affection for the 'Grand Old Man', and had as a corollary a visceral dislike of the queen—she was the only person of whom I ever heard him speak uncharitably. My own view was more sympathetic. Colin found her churlish behaviour towards Gladstone repugnant; in the light of her personal history and character, I found it explicable, if not excusable. We looked forward to arguing her out. I drafted the early chapters of the biography while Colin wrote versions of parts of the later political sections, notably on the Gladstone and Salisbury administrations, the section on the queen and the constitution, and some thoughts on the queen's mourning. And then Colin's own untimely death brought our collaboration to a halt.

More than a century after her death, Queen Victoria retains a strong grip on biographers', academics', and the public's imagination. Since this life was completed, dozens of further studies have been added to the fund of knowledge about the queen and her family. She has even starred in an episode of *Doctor Who*. No biography, especially a short one like this, can hope to encompass the full range of experience and interpretation that Victoria's life has been made to bear. Our intention in this biography was to ensure that Victoria herself was never swamped by the events in which she played a part, and to present an account of her developing personality alongside the developing role of constitutional monarchy under her reign. Victoria left huge quantities of written records, many of which have been published (though not, sadly, the journal which she kept meticulously, and which remains in the Royal Archives, having been bowdlerized by her daughter after the queen's death). It seemed important to let Victoria's own voice be heard in the biography, and the text draws extensively from her own writings.

As editor of the *Oxford Dictionary of National Biography*, Colin Matthew asked his contributors to be 'liberal, firm, and just' in their approach to their subjects. In the interests of justice, I trust that my liberality towards the queen has not outweighed his firmness. In a small way, I hope it does honour also to the memory of a great scholar, teacher, and friend.

K. D. Reynolds
February 2007

About the authors

K. D. Reynolds was a Research Editor at the *Oxford Dictionary of National Biography* from 1993 to 2003. She is the author of *Aristocratic Women and Political Society in Victorian Britain* (1998).

H. C. G. Matthew was the founding editor of the *Oxford Dictionary of National Biography*, Professor of Modern History at Oxford University, and a Fellow of St Hugh's College, Oxford. He was editor of *The Gladstone Diaries* (1972–94) and author of *Gladstone, 1809–1898* (1997).

'Herald of a new future'

Victoria (1819–1901),

queen of the United Kingdom of Great Britain and Ireland, and empress of India, was born on 24 May 1819 at Kensington Palace, London. She was the only legitimate child of the fourth son of King George III, Edward Augustus, duke of Kent (1767–1820), who in 1818 had abandoned Julie de St Laurent, his mistress of many years, in order to join his brothers in the attempt to provide an heir to the throne. His wife was a young widow: born Princess Victoire of Saxe-Coburg-Saalfeld (1786–1861), she had married the prince of Leiningen, with whom she had two children, Prince Charles and Princess Feodore, before his death in 1814. Among the duchess's brothers were Ernest, duke of Saxe-Coburg-Saalfeld, who was the father of the future prince consort, and the future king of the Belgians Leopold I (1790–1865), who had been the husband of Princess Charlotte of Wales. Charlotte's death in 1817 had precipitated the efforts to produce a new heir for the throne. Unsubstantiated rumours that Victoria was not her father's child surface periodically.

Conflict with George IV

Relationships between the duke and duchess of Kent and the court of King George IV determined the character of the princess's early years. Tension between Kent and his eldest brother spilled over at the infant's baptism on 24 June 1819, when at the last moment the prince regent as godfather refused to allow her to be named Victoire Georgiana Alexandrina Charlotte Augusta after her mother and godparents, but he eventually agreed to Alexandrina Victoria (after her godfather, the tsar of Russia, and her mother). By December 1819 deteriorating relations with the regent and ever-increasing debts led Kent to leave London, and the court. Determined to stay in England because he was convinced that his daughter would inherit the throne, Kent took his family to a house in Sidmouth, Devon; there, most unexpectedly, he died on 23 January 1820, less than a week before his father. Under his will Alexandrina Victoria, now fourth in line to the throne, was left to the sole guardianship of her mother.

The duchess of Kent shared her late husband's conviction that their daughter would one day become queen, and was determined that she should be brought up as an English princess. Not a very wise woman (and widely regarded as a stupid foreigner), the duchess was greatly under the influence of the controller of her household and former equerry to the duke, Sir John Conroy. Conroy harboured great ambitions for himself and his family, and viewed the little princess as his route to power and influence. His advice reinforced the duchess's difficulties with the rest of the royal family, and they isolated Victoria from the morally contaminated court of her 'wicked uncles'. George IV initially refused to modify his dislike of Kent's widow; he did not regard Victoria as his eventual heir, for the duke of Clarence seemed likely to pre-empt her claim by producing a legitimate child. The king would not even help to relieve their disastrous finances, leaving them to the care of Prince Leopold, until parliament in 1825 made an annual grant to the princess as heir presumptive. Even when it became clear that Victoria was likely to inherit the throne, George showed little interest in the family; it was her half-sister, Feodore, who caught his attention (and was for a time spoken of as a possible bride for the aged king).

The duchess of Kent made something of a virtue of necessity, keeping Victoria away from the court even when relations defrosted slightly, thus ensuring that the public would not see Victoria as infected by the dissolute regime of the late Hanoverian monarchy. The king invited them to Windsor for the first time when Victoria was six; she retained a strong memory of the event, and recalled in 1872 that the king had taken her by the hand, saying 'Give me your little paw' (*Letters*, 1st ser., 1.16). He was persuaded to permit his sister-in-law and niece to reside in apartments in Kensington Palace, and it was there that the princess spent her childhood.

Education of a princess

Looking back, Victoria often commented on how solitary she had been. True, the princess had little company of her own age: her half-sister, Feodore, was twelve years her senior (and married in 1828), and her only surviving cousins, Prince George of Cumberland and Prince George of

Cambridge (Princess Mary of Cambridge was not born until 1833), were kept away from her. Sir John Conroy encouraged the duchess in isolating her daughter; his own daughters, Victoire and Elizabeth Jane, provided her only regular—and increasingly unwelcome—companionship. She amused herself instead with an extensive family of dolls and animals. Dash, a King Charles spaniel, a gift from Conroy to the duchess in 1833, was the first in a long line of beloved little dogs. Other carefully vetted children were occasionally brought to play with Victoria, but friendship was out of the question with a princess who from infancy had been given a firm sense of her high position (although not of her ultimate destiny). A much quoted anecdote has the princess tell a child about to play with her toys, 'You must not touch those, they are mine; and I may call you Jane, but you must not call me Victoria' (Longford, 28).

Although she lacked companionship, Victoria was never alone. From her birth she was surrounded by devoted attendants, servants, and teachers; she never walked downstairs without someone holding her hand, and famously she never slept alone until she succeeded to the throne; instead she shared a bed with her mother. Her earliest attendants were her nurse Mrs Brock (although most unusually for the time and her class she was not put to a wet-nurse but was fed by her mother), her mother's lady-in-waiting Baroness Späth, and Princess Feodore's governess, Louise Lehzen. Lehzen, the daughter of a Lutheran pastor from Hanover, was among Victoria's most important formative influences, setting herself in opposition to Conroy and the duchess, whom she considered weak. Lehzen's ideal of a queen was Elizabeth I (1533–1603), and she imbued in Victoria a sense of the importance of strength of will, elevating her natural obstinacy and stubbornness to a principle. Lehzen, who was the princess's constant preceptress until she came to the throne, would read to Victoria morning and evening, while she was being dressed or prepared for bed, thereby helping to instil the rigid work discipline which served Victoria well throughout her life.

Contrary to her own later recollections, Victoria's formal education began before she was four, when the Revd George Davys (later bishop of Peterborough) became her tutor. From April 1823 he went regularly to Kensington Palace, where he taught Victoria the basic skills of literacy and numeracy, and gave religious instruction. Like that of most girls at this time, Victoria's early education was dominated by the writings of the evangelical moralist Mrs Trimmer, but with Davys and Lehzen she also studied history, geography, natural history, poetry, and (by 1828) Latin. Despite her future destiny, Victoria never experienced the classical education that was the shared intellectual heritage of the men of the political classes: the requirements of femininity were not to be subordinated to the needs of the state. Nor was Victoria to be a Renaissance woman like Elizabeth I, educated to write poetry as well as to embroider, to muse philosophically as well as to direct the affairs of her family. Yet her education was thorough and intensive—by 1829 she was spending five hours a day, six days a week, in formal lessons—and it stood her in good stead. French, German, and Italian were added to her curriculum. (English was always spoken in Kensington Palace, despite the preponderance of German-speakers; Davys commented on the princess's German accent, which he helped to eradicate.)

She began to study the 'female accomplishments' with a succession of tutors: playing the piano and singing with Mrs Mary Anderson and John Sale, painting and drawing with Richard Westall RA, and, with Madame Bourdin, dancing, in which she took a particular delight.

In 1830 the duchess of Kent invited the bishops of London and Lincoln to examine her daughter, and to comment on her education so far. The bishops' verdict was positive, and the duchess was publicly commended. Shortly after this examination the princess was allowed to learn of her probable future destiny. Keeping the information from her had been a kindness in the light of the uncertainty of the succession, and although some doubted whether she could have been as ignorant as was claimed, Victoria herself endorsed Lehzen's account of the way she was told. A genealogical table was inserted in her history book for her to study; 'I see I am nearer the throne than I thought ... I will be good', she said. 'I cried much on learning it, and ever deplored the contingency', she commented later (Martin, 1.13).

Conroy and the 'Kensington system'

After the examination Victoria's lessons were relieved by regular visits to the theatre and the opera. This latter was the princess's passion, and she now acquired her lifelong love of the bel canto operas of Bellini, Donizetti, and Rossini. She was even star-struck: the soprano Giulia Grisi always remained her ideal type of the singer, and she idolized the ballerina Marie Taglioni. Luigi Lablache, the bass baritone whom she first heard at a private recital in 1834, became the princess's singing teacher in 1836, beginning a relationship that lasted twenty years.

If Victoria's childhood resembled a moral and improving tale for young women, her teenage years approached melodrama. Victoria herself was the oppressed heroine, supported by her faithful retainer Lehzen, with the duchess of Kent as wicked (step)mother, the willing tool of Sir John Conroy, the 'Arch-Fiend'. Walk-on parts were played by the new king, William IV, as the choleric but kindly uncle, and the duke of Cumberland (the next heir) as the off-stage bogeyman. Victoria later recast her memories, painting her entire youth in gloomy colours and seeking to absolve her mother from all responsibility as, like herself, a victim of an all-powerful, all-malignant Conroy. Yet the duchess was no dupe, and concurred willingly in Conroy's actions: she was no less ambitious than he to wield the authority of her daughter's crown.

Conroy's influence had been tempered by the irregular but commanding presence of the duchess's brother Prince Leopold. Then in 1830 Leopold accepted the throne of Belgium. He remained in regular correspondence with both his sister and niece, but his absence enhanced the position of Conroy, whom Victoria came to loathe as 'the Monster and demon Incarnate' (Hudson, 153).

From 1830 onwards the duchess and Conroy implemented what was termed the 'Kensington system'. Their aim was to ensure that Victoria was totally dependent on them, and would not look to others for advice when she came to the throne. The duchess was appointed regent in the event of

William IV dying before Victoria reached eighteen, and Conroy's aim was to get the princess to agree to appoint him her private secretary. There was thus a practical, political reason for keeping Victoria away from the court, where she might find other advisers, and away from society, in which she might find alternative sources of support. The Kensington system was, however, more than an exercise in ambition: the aim was to make Victoria herself popular and ensure the survival of the monarchy. The Britishness of her education and upbringing was to be stressed, while her youth and purity marked her out as the herald of a new future, distanced from the moral and political corruption of the British *ancien régime*.

Beginning in 1830, Conroy and the duchess staged a series of royal progresses (directly imitating those of Elizabeth I), ostensibly to show the princess some of the historic sites of her country but in practice to bring her before the public eye and to assert her position as the heir to the throne. They succeeded: large crowds gathered to see the princess wherever she was taken, local dignitaries presented loyal addresses, and, until the enraged William IV stepped in to prevent it, guns were fired in salute. Victoria herself became increasingly unhappy about these progresses, which became more frequent and exhausting as she neared her eighteenth birthday and William IV's health began to fail.

In 1835 Victoria became seriously ill at Ramsgate. While she was in her sickbed, Conroy unsuccessfully attempted to force her to sign a document making him her private secretary when she became queen. Conroy believed she could be bullied and hectored into compliance, while the duchess applied a none-too-subtle mixture of commands, threats, and emotional blackmail. In this they misread Victoria's character completely. Strong-willed, intelligent, emotionally sensitive, lonely, with a fierce temper kept firmly in check, the young Victoria had a deep sense of duty and obligation instilled in her by Lehzen, and also a profound sense of propriety. A feeling that she was a pawn in a game being played by Conroy, who did not even treat her with courtesy, aroused all the princess's stubborn hostility and enabled her to resist her mother's demands. A little kindness and consultation, together with an acknowledgement that she was not without power, always went a long way with Victoria.

William IV's court

Victoria was not alone in her dislike for Conroy and the Kensington system. The most important opponent of Conroy and the duchess was the king himself. William IV and Queen Adelaide were fond of their niece, and in the 1820s had a better relationship with the duchess of Kent than most of the rest of the royal family. On coming to the throne, William acknowledged Victoria as his probable successor and approved the appointment of the duchess as her regent. He hoped that the princess would become a regular visitor to his court, and indeed on 24 February 1831 Victoria made her first appearance at her aunt's drawing-room (these were formal occasions at which ladies were presented and received at court; men were received at the king's levees). But the isolationism of the Kensington system demanded otherwise, and the duchess deeply offended the king by refusing to allow her daughter to attend his coronation. Further disputes about the composition of the princess's entourage followed, and the king ordered Conroy to leave Victoria's confirmation service at the Chapel Royal in St James's Palace on 30 July 1834. At a dinner in August 1836 William IV publicly insulted the duchess, who was sitting next to him, as he announced his intention to live another nine months solely to thwart her plans for a regency:

> I should then have the satisfaction of leaving the royal authority to the personal exercise of that young lady...and not in the hands of a person now near me, who is surrounded by evil advisers and who is herself incompetent to act with propriety in the station in which she would be placed. (Charlot, 68)

The king sought to free Victoria from Conroy and her mother when she came of age by offering her an independent income and household. The duchess of Kent dictated the refusal which Victoria sent, but the king recognized the mother's voice, and exonerated the princess from blame. On her eighteenth birthday, 24 May 1837, Victoria noted in the journal which she had kept since 1832, 'I shall from this day take the *firm* resolution to study with renewed assiduity, to keep my attention always on whatever I am about, and to strive to become every day less trifling and more fit for what, if Heaven wills it, I'm some day to be!' (*Girlhood*, 1.190). That evening she attended a ball at St James's before returning to Kensington through the thronged streets: 'the anxiety of the people to see poor stupid me was very great, and I must say I am quite touched by it, and feel proud which I always have done of my country and of the English nation' (ibid., 1.191). The king had not been at the ball, as he was ill in bed. Time was fast running out for the Kensington system.

'The burdens of majesty'

Accession

King William IV survived for another month, before finally succumbing on 20 June 1837. Lord Conyngham (the lord chamberlain) and William Howley (the archbishop of Canterbury) were dispatched at once to Kensington Palace to bring the news to the new queen. Victoria was summoned from her bed by her mother at six in the morning to receive them, which she did '(only in my dressing gown), and *alone*' (*Girlhood*, 1.196). That characteristic emphasis pointed to the total and immediate failure of the Kensington system as far as it concerned the ambitions of its progenitors: Conroy was immediately banished from the royal presence, and although the duchess was regularly called upon to attend her daughter in public, she was systematically excluded from all the new queen's decisions and counsels.

But in its wider aims the Kensington system bore instant fruit in the widespread popularity of the new queen. The hagiographical accounts of universal popular acclaim for Victoria were undoubtedly exaggerated: radicals, republicans, and the huge masses of the indifferent certainly did not see her as their saviour, or the monarchy as the guardian of British liberty. But, primed by the careful publicity of the previous years, the political classes were swept up in a fever of curiosity about the new queen, and for a few weeks her smallest actions were recorded, analysed, and discussed, and her public appearances were attended by vast, good-humoured crowds. Those who came into direct contact with the queen at this time had little but praise for her charm, her graciousness, her willingness to be happy, her sheer pleasure in her position, and even her appearance. Although the adjective 'lovely' was much in evidence, no one could seriously describe her as beautiful: with her lack of chin, her small mouth, and her rather prominent blue eyes, she bore a close resemblance to her unlovely Hanoverian forebears. The queen was constantly spoken of in diminutives at this time ('her little majesty', 'the little queen'), and even when fully grown she was only 4 feet 11 inches tall, and in extreme age lost several inches. She was also already tending towards the traditional stoutness of her family, although it took some years and nine children before she achieved her unmistakable 'pepper pot' silhouette. Her voice, on the other hand, was praised from the outset for its melodious quality: 'as sweet as a Virginia nightingale's', rhapsodized one American observer (E. Boykin, ed., *Victoria, Albert, and Mrs Stevenson*, 1957, 107).

Much play was made with the burdens of majesty heaped on the small shoulders of an inexperienced, unprotected girl. David Wilkie's painting *The First Council of Queen Victoria*, painted in 1837, contrasts the white-clad Victoria with the sombrely dressed, bewhiskered, elderly members of her government. The picture was inaccurate in several respects—Victoria was actually dressed in mourning for her uncle at the council on the first day of her reign—but the contrast between the masculine world of politics and the femininity of the queen was valid. It was not, however, Victoria's inexperience and fragility that impressed those present so much as her presence of mind, dignity, and courage.

Although curiosity about the queen was universal among the political classes, intense party factionalism meant that whigs and tories responded rather differently to the new reign. Seen from a long-term perspective, the monarchy's political power was slipping by comparison with that of parliament and the cabinet. But from the standpoint of the 1830s many of the precedents limiting the sovereign's power were recent and susceptible to challenge from a new monarch. The monarchy's patronage powers were considerable: a new reign might entail a new distribution. The whigs were in office in 1837, but had never had the real support of William IV. Victoria's accession offered them hope for the first time of receiving the active favour of the monarch, for the duchess of Kent and Sir John Conroy were known to support the whigs, and Victoria was supposed to have been raised a whig. The same facts caused the tories to despair: the support they had enjoyed from the monarch and their virtual monopoly on power since 1760 seemed to be at an end. The queen's intense and close relationship with her first prime minister, Lord Melbourne, lent credence to tory fears and whig hopes.

Learning to be queen: Lady Flora and the bedchamber crisis

Victoria herself greeted the news of her accession with the characteristic reflection that:

> I shall do my utmost to fulfil my duty towards my country; I am very young and perhaps in many, though not in all things, inexperienced, but I am sure, that very few have more real good will and more real desire to do what is fit and right than I have. (*Girlhood*, 1.196)

Melbourne was with the queen by 9 a.m. on 20 June, and was informed that he was to remain prime minister. She found him sympathetic, her initial assessment of him as 'a very straightforward, honest, clever and good man' (ibid., 1.197) remained unchanged, and her attachment to him deepened with time. Melbourne's constant attendance on the queen and his obvious affection for her earned her the nickname Mrs Melbourne, but although their relationship had an air of romance about it, Melbourne was more father figure than potential lover. Despite his rather lurid past, Melbourne was in many respects the ideal minister, counsellor, and private secretary for the young queen; his scholarly mind and fund of learning supplied the theoretical and practical answers to her questions about her position, and his wide experience of aristocratic and royal society, men, women, and manners was invaluable for one who had lived as secluded a life as the queen. 'Lord M. says...' was a constant refrain in her journal until 1840.

Victoria was not a complete political innocent in 1837. Her first mentor was her uncle Leopold, who on her fourteenth birthday began her political education with a dissertation on the character necessary for a monarch in an era when 'the transition from sovereign power to *absolute want* has become as frequent as sudden' (*Letters*, 1st ser., 1.46): he urged her to spend some time each day in quiet reflection and self-examination, to avoid vanity and selfishness, and to distinguish carefully between the important and the trifling. Over the next four years he regularly discussed current (especially foreign) affairs with her and advised her about reading: history and historical memoirs would enable an isolated princess to learn about the world and thus avoid being imposed on by 'wicked and designing people, particularly at a period when party spirit runs so high' (ibid., 1.48). By 1837, when it was obvious that his niece's succession to the throne his wife had been born to occupy was close, Leopold's advice came thick and fast, and much of it had a lasting impact on Victoria. He impressed on her the value of listening to the conversation of clever and informed people at dinners and social gatherings, of prudence and discretion, of support for the established church and generally conservative (though not tory) principles. Although Victoria occasionally resented the energetic interference of her uncle, Leopold gave her enough early guidance and backbone to take on her new position with something approaching equanimity. Moreover, in June 1837 he sent his own confidential adviser, Baron Christian Stockmar, to act as a friend at court for the new queen; he remained there for fifteen months, until disquiet about foreigners' influence over the queen sent him back to Coburg.

Praised and admired in her reign's honeymoon months, Victoria blossomed in her new role and threw herself with energy into learning her profession, and into the novel social whirl of balls, theatre, opera, dinners, and confidential chats with the attentive Melbourne. For the first time in more than three generations Britain had a young monarch and a lively court. Victoria relished the contrast between her oppressed youth and her new position. The coronation was held on 28 June 1838, and, while much of the lengthy ceremonial was ineptly performed (the ancient Lord Rolle tripped and rolled down the steps when paying homage to the queen), the large crowds that turned out to see the queen were enthusiastic. 'Their good-humour and excessive loyalty was beyond everything, and I really cannot say *how* proud I feel to be the Queen of *such* a *Nation*', Victoria recorded in her journal (*Girlhood*, 1.357).

But the adulation did not last long. In accordance with tradition, the ministry of the day was responsible for forming the queen's household as well as her government, and Melbourne surrounded the queen exclusively with active whig partisans. Not only her officials and attendants but also the society which gathered at the court was dominated by the whig aristocracy. By the end of the first year of her reign the tories considered Victoria 'the queen of the whigs'. Attacks on the government began to include attacks on the queen; she came to view the tories as her enemies and clung even more closely to Melbourne.

The dangers of a party-political court surfaced in the Lady Flora Hastings affair, which broke out in February 1839. The unmarried Lady Flora, the duchess of Kent's lady-in-waiting and a member of a prominent tory family, was suspected of being pregnant by Conroy. In fact, she was suffering from a tumour on her liver, and died in agony on 5 July. But before the nature of her illness became known, rumours flew about the court, medical examiners were called in, and the affair became public. The Hastings family fanned the flames of hostility towards the queen, who had not acted to quench the gossip or protect the reputation of Lady Flora. Victoria's popularity took a considerable blow—she was, after all, supposed to stand for a new, moral court, and the Lady Flora affair smacked of the old Hanoverian scandals—and she was hissed by two aristocratic ladies as she drove to Ascot on 7 June.

On 7 May 1839, in the midst of the Flora Hastings controversy, Melbourne resigned. Victoria responded with an 'agony of grief and despair' (Charlot, 141). He was not only her minister; he was her friend. The tories she considered her enemies, and she had a particular horror of the probable new prime minister, Sir Robert Peel, whose lack of social graces made the contrast with Melbourne unbearable. Melbourne's advice to the distraught queen was sound: she must accept the tories as her ministers and try to shed her dislike for Peel. She should safeguard her prerogatives, but be seen to be scrupulously fair. But he also put in her mind the idea that she might keep her household as it was, and when Peel requested changes among the ladies of her household, Victoria baulked. The ladies made a convenient sticking point for Victoria, but possibly also for Peel, who perhaps had less relish for the task of forming a minority government than his party supposed. The queen maintained that the ladies were domestic appointments, that they had no political influence, and that the precedents required no changes. Peel argued that the exclusively whig female court signalled that his government lacked the queen's confidence. If changes were not made, he could not form a government. 'Was Sir Robert so weak that *even* the ladies must be of his opinion?' (*Letters*, 1st ser., 1.209), asked the queen. Melbourne had stayed away from the palace during these negotiations, but Victoria had written him almost hourly accounts of events, and now she sent for him to tell him of Peel's demands. Melbourne called a cabinet meeting, which formally advised her to refuse changes to her household. (Here, if nowhere else, Melbourne acted unconstitutionally: until Peel declined the commission to form a government, Melbourne had no authority to advise the queen.) The attempt to form a tory ministry over, Victoria rejoiced in Melbourne's resumption of office, and in the retention of the ladies who were supporting her through the later, and most trying, stages of the Lady Flora affair.

The 'bedchamber crisis' has been ascribed to the hysterical tantrum of a young and inexperienced woman, but at the time some viewed it as an ill-omened attempt to reassert the political power of monarchy over ministers. In fact, it was something in between: the already overwrought Victoria certainly responded emotionally in this crisis, but in resisting her ministers she was testing the limits of her power. As it was obvious, even to Victoria, that the whigs could not be kept in power indefinitely, the principal result of the crisis was to confirm the widespread view that an unmarried girl on the throne was a loose cannon.

Victoria and Albert

3

Marriage and motherhood

Since marriage with a commoner was thought undesirable (though not, in Britain, illegal) the pool of Victoria's possible spouses was restricted to the protestant princes of Germany, the Netherlands, and Scandinavia, and (a remote possibility) the Orthodox princes of Russia. A great dynastic marriage was unnecessary, even unwanted: by 1840 uniting disparate countries by marriage between their hereditary rulers was a thing of the past. Possible consorts had been suggested for her since she was a tiny child, among them her cousins Prince George of Cambridge and Prince George of Cumberland. King Leopold had long ago determined to promote another Coburg alliance—between Victoria and her cousin Prince Albert of Saxe-Coburg and Gotha (1819–1861)—and had been supervising the education of his motherless nephew as a potential consort.

Victoria was alerted to the intention, and Albert and his brother Ernest were brought to Britain in May 1836 to be scrutinized. Eager to frustrate the duchess of Kent's plans,

King William IV favoured a match with Prince Alexander of Orange, and invited him to Britain with his brother also in May 1836, but he was not a success with Victoria, and nothing more was heard of that match. Albert, on the other hand, came with the blessing of Uncle Leopold, and Victoria was more or less determined to find him pleasing. His physical attractions did much to outweigh his tendency to fall asleep during evening parties, and the cousins kept up a correspondence over the next few years. But the engagement which Albert had been led to expect was slow to materialize. Once on the throne, Victoria relished her independence. Even the scandals of 1839 failed to persuade her that marriage was a solution to her difficulties. On 15 July (ten days after Lady Flora's death) she told Leopold that there was no prospect of her marrying Albert for at least two or three years: she had a '*great* repugnance to change my present position' (*Letters*, 1st ser., 1.224). A visit from the Coburg brothers was nevertheless scheduled for the autumn, and on 10 October they arrived at Windsor. Watching them arrive from the top of the stairs, Victoria fell in love. 'It was with some emotion that I beheld Albert—who is *beautiful*', she told her journal (*Girlhood*, 2.262). On 15 October she undertook the somewhat awkward task of proposing to Albert, saying 'it would make me *too happy* if he would consent to what I wished (to marry me)' (ibid., 2.268). Albert accepted.

Albert was far from a popular choice of consort. In some quarters he was viewed as a penniless foreign adventurer, coming to Britain to burden its taxpayers. Moreover, he was slightly younger than the queen, and part of the purpose of encouraging her marriage was to place the inexperienced, wilful girl under the tutelage of a more mature, masculine intellect. When the match was first raised with him, Melbourne objected on grounds of their consanguinity, adding 'Those Coburgs are not popular abroad; the Russians hate them.' But as Victoria herself pointed out, 'Who was there else?' (*Girlhood*, 2.153).

Marriage changed everything for Victoria. Before the wedding, on 10 February 1840 in the Chapel Royal at St James's Palace, she had been anxious to assert herself and her authority over her future husband. Albert was not permitted to select his own household (apart from a few personal retainers); his desire for an extended honeymoon in the country was rebuffed with a reminder that his wife had political duties in London; and in several ways Victoria made plain that politics were to be her preserve, not his. However, within two years Albert had moved from wielding the blotting paper on Victoria's official letters to dictating their content. He also changed her preference for the gaieties of London society to one for the relative rural quiet of Windsor, and was poised to remove from his wife's household the long-serving Baroness Lehzen (whom he loathed and regarded as an evil, and countervailing, influence with his wife).

This transformation stemmed in part from Albert's determination to reshape his wife's character and to be the master in their relationship, and in part from Victoria embracing wholeheartedly the prevalent view of the correct relationship between the sexes, and especially between husband and wife: women were by nature inferior and dependent, and it was their duty to submit to and adore their husbands. Indeed, Victoria frequently expressed her regret at the unnatural order within her own household, in which the accident of her birth and position denied Albert his rightful place at the head of all her affairs. Not that a submissive role came entirely easily. She was used to having her own way, and her fiery temper fitted uneasily with Albert's chilly rationality. There were frequent scenes: Albert preferred to deal with an argument by leaving the room, and the corridors could echo to the sound of his wife's fury. Victoria soon became accustomed to finding herself in the wrong, and blamed herself bitterly for disputing with her husband. For his part, Albert keenly felt the anomalies of his position, and determined from the outset that although he could not officially assume the male role at the head of his family's public affairs, he would be master in his own house.

Albert's dominance over Victoria became total; after his death she observed desolately that she had 'leant on him for all and everything—without whom I did nothing, moved not a finger, arranged not a print or photograph, didn't put on a gown or bonnet if he didn't approve it' (*Dearest Mama*, 23). This was the ideal of womanhood with a vengeance, and it was achieved by Albert breaking his wife's will. If she challenged him, he responded by threatening to withdraw his affection or even (on occasion) to withdraw entirely from the relationship; Victoria would respond with abject submission. Albert's patriarchy was thus achieved by treating his wife as a wilful child (in the evangelical tradition of child-rearing, the child's will had to be broken in order for it to be remade as a Christian): the 'Beloved Victoria' of his letters before their marriage soon became 'Dear Child' or 'Dear Good, Little One'. The fatherless Victoria all her life needed a strong, masculine figure to lean on. Albert was only too happy to oblige. But no doubts can be entertained about the depth of Victoria's passion for her husband. Albert made up for her childhood; he became her moral guide and teacher as well as her lover, companion, friend. She idolized him, worshipped him, and sang his praises to all who would listen. He was 'my beloved Albert', an 'Angel' (constantly), a 'perfect being' (*Letters*, 1st ser., 1.460), 'the purest and best of human beings' (ibid., 3.452). The strong-willed, stubborn, curious, sociable Victoria, whose character had been forged by the Kensington system, was transformed within years of her marriage (not without some difficulty and rebellion on her part) into a personally and intellectually submissive, almost reclusive wife by Albert's patriarchal insecurity. She loved him; she was diminished by him.

If the transformation of Albert's position owed much to his wife's temperament, it owed as much to her fertility. Within weeks of their marriage Victoria was dismayed to find herself pregnant. Although the queen was blessed with an iron constitution and her pregnancies were generally physically easy, custom—and memories of the death of her cousin Princess Charlotte in childbirth—required that she be treated as an invalid for their duration. She also suffered severely from what was later termed postnatal depression after the births of several of her children. It was during the weeks before the birth of their first child that Albert established himself *de facto* as the queen's private secretary (she had no officially appointed private secretary until 1867), and as a powerful, even dominant, voice in court politics. Victoria Adelaide was born on 21 November 1840; 'Never mind, the next will be a Prince', Victoria told her disappointed attendants (Weintraub, 149). It was: Albert Edward, prince of

Wales, was born on 9 November 1841 and was followed by Alice (1843), Alfred (1844), Helena (1846), Louise (1848), Arthur (1850), Leopold (1853), and Beatrice (1857). The queen suffered no miscarriage or stillbirth, and all her children survived to adulthood, a situation unusual even among the Victorian upper classes. During the birth of Prince Leopold the queen was given chloroform for the first time—'soothing, quieting & delightful beyond measure', said the queen (Longford, 234)—and put an end to the arguments about its general use. Victoria herself had been breastfed by her mother; her own children were promptly put out to wet-nurses. Victoria, who dreaded childbirth, recognized the political as much as the personal inconvenience of numerous offspring. These were, after all, the 'hungry forties', and radical opinion, which had commented unfavourably on Victoria's choice of a penniless husband, groaned at the biennial increases to her family.

Family values and the bourgeois monarchy

The critics were in a minority. From the birth of the princess royal in 1840 the royal couple—now a royal family—were held up as an example of domestic felicity. The irony, however, was that although the Victorians placed a high premium on the role of the wife and mother in creating ideal family life, in the royal family this was Albert's province. Despite his inroads into Victoria's public life, both he and Victoria always remained uncomfortably aware that the 'natural order' was inverted, and that Victoria reigned sovereign, while Albert's position derived exclusively from his relationship with her and, even more humiliatingly, from fathering the heir to the throne. They consciously took the decision that, in their home life at least, Albert would have the authority and rights of a traditional paterfamilias. Hence it was he, not Victoria, who (after some early arguments) was the dominant voice in determining how the children were educated and brought up, who oversaw the modernization of the royal household (managing servants was usually a female job), and who romped in the nursery with his children. Victoria was by no means an archetypal Madonna-esque mamma, her world revolving around her children: she disliked small babies—'froglike', she thought—and children were a worry. Besides, they distracted her attention from Albert and, more importantly, they distracted Albert's attention from her. Being a wife ranked high above motherhood in Victoria's priorities, and she was jealous of anyone or anything that took his attention from her. She was lucky in Albert's utter uxoriousness: his care to avoid even the semblance of interest in other women pleased Victoria, while alienating him further from British aristocratic society and the royal household.

The apocryphal story of the lady in the audience at a performance of *Antony and Cleopatra* turning to her companion and saying 'How unlike, how very unlike the home life of our own dear Queen' represents something fundamental about the impact of royal domesticity. George IV and William IV in their private lives had been bywords for lechery and irregular marital affairs; Victoria and Albert were their diametric opposites. And as the sons of George III symbolized the excesses of aristocratic behaviour, so his granddaughter came to symbolize middle-class virtue, with her family life—notably painted by Edwin Landseer—at its heart. But although the queen shared some of the tastes and values of her most respectable subjects (Lord Salisbury later declared that if he knew what the queen thought about an issue, he knew what the middle classes would think), and although in later life her deliberate shunning of the more ostentatious trappings of royalty made it easy to think of her as a bourgeois widow at the head of the family firm, she was in fact *sui generis*, one of a kind. As Arthur Ponsonby put it, 'She bore no resemblance to an aristocratic English lady, she bore no resemblance to a wealthy middle-class Englishwoman, nor to any typical princess of a German court... she was simply without prefix or suffix "The Queen" ' (Ponsonby, 70).

A place of one's own: Osborne and Balmoral

Creating a suitable setting for this idyllic family life took up much royal energy in the 1840s and 1850s. Victoria had inherited three royal residences with the crown: Buckingham Palace, Windsor Castle, and the Brighton Pavilion. All had disadvantages: Albert disliked London life, which made him ill; at Windsor there were no private grounds (the public had admission to all the gardens and park, and the family were on constant display); and the Brighton Pavilion was hedged in by suburban development. Added to which, all three were, as crown property, under the control of the Office of Woods and Forests, which inhibited changes to the buildings that would make them suit their needs and taste.

The need for a home of their own became pressing. The major role in imagining, designing, and executing the building of the royal houses most closely associated with

Victoria—Balmoral Castle on Deeside in Aberdeenshire, and Osborne House, near Cowes on the Isle of Wight—was Albert's, with Victoria an uncritical admirer of his achievements. Albert's taste in matters architectural inevitably dominated: he, after all, had travelled, had been in Italy as well as his native Germany, while Victoria's experience, even of her own country, was limited to the tours Sir John Conroy had planned, and the childhood trips to the south coast for her health. In September 1842 the royal couple made their first visit to Scotland, keeping great state in Edinburgh (but not on the scale of George IV's famous Scottish jaunt of 1822), and then visiting in slightly less state some grandees of the lowlands and southern highlands. It was, 'Albert says very German-looking' (*Leaves from the Journal*, 13). There could be no higher praise, and Victoria's love affair with Scotland, which long survived her husband, began.

A summer cruise around the south coast and across to France and Belgium in 1843 reminded Victoria of her pleasant seaside holidays as a child, and she and Albert began to look for a seaside retreat. The Osborne estate near Cowes on the Isle of Wight was for sale, and after a preliminary visit in October 1844 they completed the purchase in November 1845. Even before this, Albert began an ambitious programme of building, and he and Victoria visited Osborne seven times in 1845 to familiarize themselves with their new home and to oversee progress on the building site. An Italianate palace replaced the original eighteenth-century Osborne House with remarkable speed: the old house was demolished in May 1845, and Victoria and Albert moved in during September 1846, although the building was not complete until 1849. Victoria was delighted with the house: it offered distance from the annoyances of London and politics, privacy, serenity, space for family life. More importantly, it was a 'place of *one's own*' (*Letters*, 1st ser., 2.41). And it was all Albert's work: 'I get fonder and fonder of it, one is so quiet here, and everything is of interest, it being so completely my beloved one's creation—his delight and pride', she wrote (Duchess of York, *Victoria and Albert: Life at Osborne House*, 1988, 117). Albert relaxed at Osborne, and occupied himself with estate improvement, building, and playing with the children while Victoria sketched and painted in watercolours and admired everything he did. Courtiers and ministers were less enamoured of the domestic idyll on the island: there was no room in Osborne for a large entourage, and staff and courtiers were out-housed around the estate, while ministers found the distance from London inconvenient for the execution of public business. But the royal couple discovered that even a few miles of sea were insufficient protection from the intrusions of the curious and the demands of their position: Scotland called them.

Victoria and Albert returned to Scotland in 1844 to stay with the duke and duchess of Atholl at Blair Castle, Perthshire, and again in 1847, this time as part of a yachting tour. Their pleasure was dimmed by wet weather, and on learning that the east coast, and Deeside in particular, had a better climate, Victoria and Albert decided to look there for a Scottish home. They purchased Balmoral, sight unseen, in August 1848 and rebuilt it between 1853 and 1855. Balmoral provided privacy in abundance and, for Victoria, a kind of freedom unavailable elsewhere: 'The Queen is running in and out of the house all day long, and often goes about alone, walks into the cottages and sits down and chats with the old women', Charles Greville reported (Charlot, 290). Victoria delighted in the frank conversation of the high-landers. Influenced by her love of Walter Scott's novels, she saw highlanders as noble peasants, with none of the cringing servility, corrupted manners, and predatory impertinence of southerners. They seemed to stand outside the usual British class structure: she thought them a colourful feudal rem-nant rather than an agricultural proletariat, enjoyed their theatricality, and granted them a licence not permitted to any others of her subjects.

Victoria and Albert embraced Scottishness wholeheartedly. Balmoral was bedecked in tartan, the children were dressed in kilts, and the whole family took to highland pursuits. They made expeditions (some in transparent incognito) to local beauty spots, climbed and rode in the mountains, attended the local highland games, and rowed on the loch. Albert studied Gaelic, hunted, shot, and fished; Victoria followed, often taking her sketchbooks with her. When even Balmoral seemed too crowded, too urban, Victoria and Albert retreated to the remodelled shiels (stone huts), for-merly used by the gillies, at Alt-na Giuthasach, some 5 miles from the castle, for greater solitude and simplicity. Solitude was relative: their party included a maid of honour, two maids, a valet, a footman, a cook, Albert's Jäger, and 'old John Gordon and his wife' (*Leaves from the Journal*, 112). The annual autumn train journey to Balmoral (Victoria first travelled by train in 1842) was eagerly awaited by the royal family; the royal household were less enthralled at the prospect of weeks of isolation in the chilly north, while the ministers required to be in attendance, far from

Westminster, seldom comfortable, and often unwelcome, tended to greet news of their duty with dismay. But the convenience of politicians was of no interest to the queen: 'Really', she wrote, 'when one is so happy & blessed in one's home life, as I am, Politics (provided my country is safe) must take only a 2nd place' (Longford, 184).

The quest for political stability

Moving on from Melbourne

The fall of the Melbourne government in 1841 was a personal and political blow to the queen. Under Melbourne she had developed from an isolated, quietly rebellious child into an eager, imperious young woman. She had thoroughly established her independence from her mother and her mother's agents: by 1841 she was beginning to forgive the duchess of Kent for her childhood, and to establish a more amicable relationship with her. Albert's arrival at her side in 1840 ensured that the lessons of her early errors did not go unheeded: that gossip leads to slander, and too much fraternizing with courtiers endangered the dignity of the queen; and that while the ministry served at the queen's pleasure, the queen was to find her pleasure in accordance with the will of the electorate.

Even before the return of a tory majority in the House of Commons in September 1841, Melbourne began preparing the ground for his inevitable departure, offering sound advice to Victoria on her constitutional duty towards her ministers, of whatever political complexion. With Albert and Albert's private secretary, George Anson, Melbourne began a series of secret negotiations with Sir Robert Peel over the composition of the queen's household to avoid a repetition of the 'bedchamber crisis': the queen could not be seen to back down and remove her ladies at the demand of the prime minister, but Peel still needed to be able to show that the female household was not dominated by his enemies. It was arranged that three ladies would offer their resignations without being asked and would be replaced with less overtly political women, thereby saving face all round. But, despite the months of careful preparation, Victoria was desolated by Melbourne's departure, and Melbourne (similarly distressed) agreed to continue their correspondence. Although Melbourne's letters urged the queen to have confidence in Peel and to comply with the ministry, the correspondence was strictly unconstitutional, as it meant that the monarch was secretly receiving information and advice from the opponents of her ministers. Had it become widely known, the exchange would have amounted to a public declaration of her lack of confidence in her government. Despite intervention from Baron Stockmar the correspondence continued unabated through 1842, and diminished only when Melbourne's health collapsed and the queen thoroughly let go of the past.

The constitution, according to Stockmar, gave 'the Sovereign in his functions a deliberative part' (Letters, 1st ser., 1.352–3), that is to say, the queen's constitutional role was to reflect on the policies, persons, and practices of her ministers, and after due consideration to give her opinion to her ministers, expecting it to be heard and heeded. Her prerogatives were to be observed rigorously, and in return she would support her ministers publicly and endorse their decisions. Stockmar doubted whether the queen possessed the means to carry out this deliberative role, an assessment which belittled both Victoria's intellect and her character. Certainly the queen needed political advisers, yet the constitution hindered her from obtaining them, as theoretically the monarch should be advised only by her ministers, and particularly by her prime minister. From her ministers she would hear only one side of an argument, restricting her capacity to deliberate on the issues. If she could not receive advice from the opposition, where was she to turn? A king might expect his court to provide an additional source of political information, from among the lords-in-waiting with seats in parliament, and the great officers of his household, or from friends of his youth. This route was closed to Victoria because her closest attendants were all women and because after the 'bedchamber crisis' it became expedient to disengage the entire household from politics. And she had no friends from her childhood. Educated in isolation, and a girl to boot, she had no network of acquaintances in the political world and restricted contacts even with aristocratic society: when she came to make appointments to her household, she was forced to rely on hearsay accounts of the agreeable qualities of different ladies or, as time passed, to select her attendants from among the families of people already in her service. So the queen had a small pool of resources on which to draw: King Leopold and Stockmar, Albert and his secretary Anson, and ultimately her own judgement. Her judgement generally found that reliance on Albert in all political matters would produce the best results.

An account of Victoria's political opinions and actions from her marriage until Albert's death, then, is largely an account of Albert's. Slowed down by her frequent pregnancies and constrained by her acceptance of the inferiority of women's capabilities and her own education and intellect, she gave the function of deliberation to Albert. Fitted by sex, by temperament, and by training, Albert was king in all but name. 'Oh! if only I could make him king', Victoria exclaimed (Longford, 179). It was the one thing she could not do for him. The years between 1840 and 1861 have often been described as a period of 'dual monarchy': Albert took on the executive, deliberative role, while Victoria took the more dignified part (to use Walter Bagehot's term) and provided legitimacy for Albert's executive. She worked hard at the official papers, discussing them with Albert every morning and corresponding with and interviewing her ministers (always with Albert present); but Albert often drafted the responses, which Victoria copied out to send. In 1850 Albert summed up his interpretation of his position to the duke of Wellington: he was 'the natural head of her family, superintendent of her household, manager of her private affairs, sole *confidential* adviser in politics, and only assistant in her communications with the officers of the Government, ... the private secretary of the sovereign and her permanent minister' (Martin, 2.260).

Unlike Melbourne, Albert was not subject to the vagaries of the electorate, and he had no political interests to serve that were not Victoria's. The monarchy, in Albert's and Stockmar's formulation, was to be politically neutral. Neutrality meant not taking sides in party-political disputes; it meant considering a question from all sides and promoting the national interest, not the short-term interests of political parties bent on gaining and retaining power. It did not mean forgoing a political function for the monarchy. If anything, it elevated the importance of the monarch's political voice: 'Is the sovereign not the natural guardian of the honour of his country, is he not *necessarily* a politician?', Albert reflected (Connell, 142). In the early Victorian state Albert was the politician in the royal family.

Victoria's conversion to Albert's way of thinking was nowhere clearer than in the transformation of her feelings about Sir Robert Peel, whose assumption of office in 1841 she had so dreaded. By 1845 his own resignation was a matter of profound regret, for he had become 'our worthy Peel ... a man of unbounded *loyalty*, *courage*, patriotism, and *high-mindedness*' (*Letters*, 1st ser., 2.75). Peel was a man after Albert's own heart: hard-working, earnest, reserved, dedicated. Through Albert's eyes Victoria came to see the merits of her prime minister, and, in his resignations over the corn laws in 1845 and 1846, recognized a disinterested service to herself and the nation that rose above the interests of party.

Above all, the domestic political agenda for Victoria and Albert was defined by a quest for political stability. Men and measures that upset the equilibrium of the country were to be deplored, and the highest praise they could heap on a minister was that he was 'safe'. A safe minister placed the needs of his country above the demands of party politics; a safe minister headed a government with a firm, controllable majority in the House of Commons, thus obviating the need for frequent, potentially tumultuous elections; a safe minister was considerate of Victoria's and Albert's feelings and position, and upheld the constitutional privileges of the monarchy.

All government business passed across Victoria's and Albert's desks; Albert's conscientiousness ensured that it all received due attention. Victoria involved herself wholeheartedly less often. The issues which caught her attention and seemed to her to be of paramount importance fell broadly into two categories: matters concerning British security and prestige, and matters concerning royal authority, prestige, and security. In the substantive domestic debates of the 1840s—over the corn laws, the effects of industrialization, the implications of organized working-class radicalism—she expressed little interest. Neither Lord Ashley's Ten Hours Act (which reduced working hours for women and children in factories) nor the agitations of the Chartists could expect sympathy from the queen.

It was not that Victoria lacked compassion. She believed profoundly in the obligations of the rich towards the poor, and dispensed large sums in personal charity: between 1837 and 1871 she gave £8160 (nearly 15 per cent of her privy purse) annually to charities (Prochaska, 77), and the figure rose thereafter. But like most of the upper classes, she regarded charity as an individual, religious duty, not a matter for government or collective action, which could damage trade and industry. She used her position to encourage others to be charitable, and became patron of some 150 institutions. She periodically issued orders that ladies appearing at court should wear gowns of British manufacture, to support native industry, while the *bal costumé* of 12 May 1842 (at which

Albert and Victoria appeared as King Edward III and Queen Philippa) was intended to provide work for the unemployed Spitalfields silk weavers. A regularly repeated calumny, that Victoria gave only £5 to the many appeals on behalf of the starving Irish during the famine years, is belied by the evidence: she headed one subscription list with a donation of £2000, made contributions to other projects brought to her attention by her ladies-in-waiting, and attended a charity performance at the opera as well as other fund-raising events. But her sympathy with the sufferings of the Irish peasantry waned rapidly when they turned to political action to improve their lot, threatening the security of her realm. The agitation in Ireland and the murders of landlords in 1847–8, coinciding with the year of revolutions on the continent, filled Victoria with foreboding for the safety of her throne; the Chartists' Kennington Common meeting of 10 April 1848, though ultimately a damp squib, sent the royal family scurrying from London to the safety of the Isle of Wight.

Provided my country is safe

Foreign affairs were Albert's greatest preoccupation, and he drew Victoria along with him. His vision was for Europe to be led by a united, liberal Germany in alliance with Britain—constitutional monarchy triumphing over the despotic monarchies of Russia, Austria, and Prussia for the general good and in the interests of international peace. Ironically, it was with Britain's hereditary enemy, France, that Victoria and Albert developed their first ties in the 1840s. Their uncle Leopold had married a daughter of the Orléanist king of the French, Louis Philippe, in

1832, and it was essentially a family visit that Victoria and Albert paid to the French royal family at the Château d'Eu, near Cherbourg, in August 1843: it was the first time an English sovereign had visited the French sovereign since 1520, and Victoria's first journey abroad. Perhaps in consequence, Victoria was in 1844 visited by no fewer than three reigning sovereigns: the king of Saxony, Tsar Nicholas I of Russia, and Louis Philippe paying a reciprocal visit, the first such since 1356. The crown prince of Prussia also visited Windsor in 1844, and in 1845 Victoria made her first journey to Germany, to see Albert's homeland of Coburg and also to visit the Prussian court in Berlin. In consequence, Victoria came increasingly to feel herself part of an international brotherhood of monarchy. She and Albert felt that their personal ties with the ruling houses of Europe gave them a special knowledge and authority in foreign affairs, an opinion which brought them into regular conflict with Lord Palmerston, who in 1846 returned to the Foreign Office.

Palmerston took a thoroughgoing whig view of the relationship between crown and parliament, and had no time for the royal couple's inflated idea of their own role. For their part, Victoria and Albert found Palmerston's policies often rash and inflammatory, and they found his unpopularity in the courts and embassies of Europe personally embarrassing. His support for liberal, constitutional causes abroad and his hostility to French interests seemed to Victoria and Albert the very opposite of desirable—not least because they undermined the position of monarchs abroad—and his habits in the matter of the dispatches, which he often sent to the royal couple only after they had been sent abroad, were at best discourteous and at worst unconstitutional. While the queen repeatedly called on her prime minister, Lord John Russell, to dismiss Palmerston, and even threatened to do so herself, Palmerston, secure in popular approval and parliamentary ascendancy, carried on blithely, though he bowed to proprieties and pulled back from the brink of open confrontation with the queen. Great were the rejoicings at court in December 1851 when Palmerston brought about his own downfall by expressing support for the new emperor of France, Napoleon III, contrary to the government's stated policy of neutrality.

The high Victorian decade: war and rebellion

Palmerston's fall crowned for Victoria a triumphant year which had been dominated by the realization of Albert's plans for the Great Exhibition. Her total faith in her husband's vision for the Crystal Palace in Hyde Park was triumphantly vindicated. The opening was, Victoria thought, 'the *greatest* day in our history, the *most beautiful* and *imposing* and *touching* spectacle ever seen' (*Letters*, 1st ser., 2.383); more importantly, it was a triumph for Albert, who at last seemed to receive the popular acclaim his wife thought he deserved. Albert still had no official status in Britain, a situation the queen considered intolerable and which she regularly pressed her ministers to remedy, to no avail.

Two events overseas engaged Victoria in a way that no peacetime incident had: the war in the Crimea, and the mutiny in India in 1857. As the first troops departed for the Crimea in 1854, she became fervently martial in spirit.

Regarding herself as head of the army, and the soldiers peculiarly her own, she watched countless soldiers depart, and when the navy set sail for the Baltic, she was aboard the royal yacht *Fairy* at Spithead: 'Navy and Nation were particularly pleased at *my leading them out*', she reported to King Leopold (*Letters*, 1st ser., 3.20). Victoria was not called on to be another Elizabeth, but she became engrossed in the distant war, seizing on dispatches and news, writing constant encouragement to her generals and to the widows of fallen officers, instigating the casting of the Crimean campaign medal, and bestowing it personally on hundreds of returning soldiers; the first such ceremony was on 18 May 1855. She helped to design the Victoria Cross, suggesting its famous motto, 'For Valour', and instituting it by royal warrant. More warlike, if that were possible, than her prime minister, Palmerston, she reluctantly acquiesced in the peace concluded in March 1856, recognizing that 'no *glory* could have been hoped for us' (ibid., 3.235) by continuing hostilities. She followed with interest and approval the activities of Florence Nightingale at Scutari, and presented her with a brooch on her return as a mark of approbation for her work among the soldiers 'whose sufferings you have had the *privilege* of alleviating in so merciful a manner' (ibid., 3.216). The queen herself visited countless wounded and sick soldiers on their return to Britain, and urged on the government the need to provide adequate hospital facilities. On 19 May 1856 she laid the foundation stone for the Royal Victoria Hospital, Netley, Hampshire, and for the rest of her life she took a keen interest in it, visiting regularly.

The war also transformed Napoleon III into Britain's closest ally. An imperial visit to Britain in May 1855 convinced

Victoria of the emperor's qualities; Empress Eugénie too met
with her approbation, for Victoria admired beauty in other
women. Victoria paid a reciprocal visit in August to her ally
in Paris, where she was '*delighted, enchanted, amused* and
interested, and think I never saw anything more *beautiful*
and gay than Paris' (*Letters*, 1st ser., 3.172), and paid a visit of
respect to the tomb of the first Napoleon. The visit sealed the
alliance, and had longer-term importance as the origin of
the prince of Wales's love of France which in a new century
brought the entente cordiale.

The country had scarcely recovered from the Crimean War
when news began filtering back to Britain of a mutiny by
sepoys serving in the East India Company's army. Victoria
was shocked by the accounts of the massacres: 'Altogether,
the whole is so much more distressing than the Crimea—
where there was *glory* and honourable warfare, and where
the poor women and children were safe', she observed
(*Letters*, 1st ser., 3.313). She received regular reports from the
governor-general, Lord Canning, and from his wife, Charlotte, who had been one of her own ladies-in-waiting. The
rebellion suppressed, the queen put herself firmly behind
Canning's policy of relative clemency towards Indians not
directly involved in the insurrection. Palmerston's government fell in February 1858, and it was Lord Derby's
second short-lived ministry which brought India under
direct British rule. Victoria required that the proclamation
made in India to inform the people of the change should
'breathe feelings of generosity, benevolence, and religious
feeling', and was especially insistent on the inclusion of a
message of religious toleration (ibid., 3.379, 389).

The fluid state of party allegiances in the 1850s meant that changes in administration were relatively frequent (and threatened changes more so). The royal prerogative of appointing ministers had not yet fallen into abeyance, and Albert in particular was active in negotiating the formation of cabinets. Palmerston's return to cabinet office under Lord Aberdeen in December 1852 effectively set the limits on royal power. He could not be kept out of the cabinet, but he accepted the Home Office rather than the Foreign Office. This became a standard approach for Victoria: rather than objecting to an individual *tout court*, she would suggest he was inappropriate for a particular office. When Aberdeen's coalition government was brought down in January 1855, Albert unsuccessfully attempted to broker new coalitions with Derby or Russell at the head, but the royal couple were forced to concede defeat and ask Palmerston to form a government.

In the context of the Crimean War, Victoria became more sympathetic to Palmerston's aims and methods: his belligerent stance enhanced British (and Victoria's) prestige. With Lord Clarendon as foreign secretary in the new ministry she had the additional reassurance that foreign affairs were in the hands of 'an able, sensible, impartial man' (Charlot, 367). Although Victoria and Albert softened their view of Palmerston during his period as prime minister, they attempted to prevent his return after the fall of Lord Derby's minority Conservative administration following the general election in June 1859. By then the European situation was critical, as Austrian rule in northern Italy came under challenge, and the court, fearing that Palmerston would be anti-Austrian, invited Lord Granville to form a ministry. On

Granville's failure to do so, Palmerston was unavoidable, as was Russell, his foreign secretary. Victoria and Albert subsequently expended much energy in mediating between Russell and Palmerston, and in insisting that Britain should not be drawn into war over Italian affairs.

Family and tragedy

An expanding family, 1841–1861

While politics, government, and foreign affairs dominated Victoria's and Albert's official, but largely unobserved, life, the affairs of their family dominated public perceptions of the royal couple. The public image of a domestic family enjoying bourgeois pursuits (albeit on a regal scale) belied the reality of the long periods of separation of the parents from their children, whose regular companions were tutors and governesses, as in most upper-class families. Victoria was not a cold, distant mother: like many mothers, she had mixed feelings towards her children. Once past babyhood, if they were attractive, moderately intelligent, and above all, well behaved, she responded well to them. She loved the idea of family life (which she had not herself experienced as a child), and was proud of her collective brood; individually, she could find them trying.

In Vicky, the princess royal, their eldest and most intellectually promising child, Victoria and particularly Albert felt a special interest, and the education of their eldest son, Albert Edward, the prince of Wales, was planned in minute detail. An inappropriate educational programme, unfavourable comparisons with his elder sister, and constant hectoring from both his parents drove the prince in precisely the direction his parents had sought to avoid. Victoria wanted Bertie, as he was known, to be the image of his upright, dutiful, morally austere, intellectual father, to become a model king, liberal, just, pure. Bertie, as soon as the opportunity presented itself, kicked over the traces and threw himself into a life of pleasure. Affie (Alfred), as the second son and heir presumptive to the dukedom of Saxe-Coburg and Gotha, also caused his parents concern, showing too much inclination to follow Bertie's example: wanting to be a sailor, he joined the navy at thirteen, and spent most of his formative years away from home. Alice, the third child, shared in some measure the interest bestowed on the elder children, but the children who followed later (Helena, Louise, Arthur, and Leopold) were unlikely to succeed to the throne, and were all too aware of their secondary importance, a position which, ironically, left their parents more freely affectionate towards them. Arthur was Victoria's favourite child, and Leopold, by virtue of his ill health, the most over-protected. Beatrice, the youngest and a bright, lively child, captured her mother's affection in a way the older children had not, and 'Baby' was indulged.

The relationship between Victoria and her eldest daughter became difficult as Vicky approached maturity. Her interests and tastes had been formed by her father, her intellectual skills were considerable, and she and Albert adored each other. Victoria felt excluded and threatened by the closeness of their relationship; Albert found his daughter more intelligent and sympathetic than his wife, and did not hesitate to scold Victoria in front of their children. Increasingly preoccupied with public affairs, he could not accept that Victoria sometimes needed his company and undivided attention. During her last pregnancy in 1856–7 the issue caused frequent disputes between them: Albert thought that with eight children his wife had sufficient resources and company, but Victoria did not find it easy to establish intimate relationships with young people, and, as she told her uncle, '*All* the numerous children are as *nothing* to me when *he* [Albert] *is away*' (*Letters*, 1st ser., 3.305).

It had long been Albert's hope that his eldest daughter should marry the heir to the Prussian throne, a project first officially mooted in 1851, when the prince and princess of Prussia visited the Great Exhibition with their son Prince Frederick William (Fritz). The alliance was to rescue Prussia—and hence Germany and all Europe—from the dangers of 'Russian reaction and French licence' (Longford, 259). In September 1855 the 24-year-old prince arrived at Balmoral to ask for the hand of the princess royal, who had not yet celebrated her fifteenth birthday, or made her début in society. Victoria and Albert approved, but required that nothing be said to Vicky until after her confirmation (to be held after Easter 1856). Fritz would then be allowed to 'make her the proposal, which, however, I have little—indeed no—doubt she will gladly *accept*' (*Letters*, 1st ser., 3.187), Victoria exulted. The queen believed that love was a precondition of marriage and had strong reservations about child brides, but she wanted Albert's hopes fulfilled and was anxious lest Fritz should be unwilling to wait for Vicky to grow up. She was, however, persuaded of Fritz's virtues and, with her own experience in mind, expected her daughter to find the young man irresistible. Vicky herself expediently allowed herself to fall in love with her suitor. The planned delay was allowed to lapse within days, and on 29 September 1855 he proposed in form and was accepted, on the understanding that no marriage could take place until after Vicky's seventeenth birthday. It now became necessary that the princess royal be treated as an adult, despite her youth. The queen veered emotionally between sorrow at the premature ending of her eldest child's childhood and her impending initiation into the world of matrimony, pride in securing the ambitious match, and irritation that Vicky now shared the precious dinners with Albert that had often become the queen's only waking time alone with her husband.

It was in the context of her children's increasing maturity that Victoria raised once more the question of Albert's official status: as matters stood, he owed his position entirely to his wife, and in the event of her early death would have only such status as his son chose to give him. An attempt to have him made prince consort by act of parliament in 1854 soon foundered, and in 1856 Victoria again attempted to have his position confirmed, but without success. Giving up on the parliamentary route, on 25 June 1857 she conferred the title of prince consort on her husband by royal letters patent.

The princess royal's wedding took place at the Chapel Royal, St James's, on 25 January 1858, Victoria having firmly quashed any suggestion that the ceremony might take place in Berlin: 'Whatever may be the usual practice of Prussian Princes, it is not *every* day that one marries the eldest daughter of the Queen of England', she declared (*Letters,*

1st ser., 3.321). Once her daughter was safely in Berlin, and officially a woman rather than a girl, Victoria found herself able to enter into the sort of confidential relationship that had previously eluded her. Her eldest daughter received a regular barrage of letters, and the correspondence flourished for forty years, punctuated by infrequent visits. Indeed, so frequently did Victoria write in the first months of Vicky's marriage, with so many demands, instructions, criticisms, and admonitions, that Baron Stockmar (who was still offering advice from Coburg) warned Albert that she would make her daughter ill. Vicky, like her mother, had soon become pregnant and in January 1859 gave birth to her first son, Victoria's first grandchild, the future Kaiser Wilhelm II, known to his family as Willie. Unlike Victoria, Vicky loved babies and small children, and the queen regularly scolded her for spending too much time in the nursery. Breastfeeding too was a practice of which Victoria disapproved strongly for women in their position—'I hoped ... she would give up nursing, as we Princesses had other duties to perform', she told one of her cousins (ibid., 3.350)— and it was to be a regular bone of contention with her daughters.

Others were leaving the schoolroom: in 1860 the prince of Wales made his first official solo tour, to Canada and the United States, where he was greeted with enthusiasm. Prince Alfred had already gone to sea in 1858. Princess Alice's future was settled in November 1860, when she became engaged to the rather stolid Prince Louis of Hesse, Victoria having taken advantage of Vicky's vantage point at the heart of protestant Europe to assess potential marriage partners for her other children. Vicky also vetted possible brides for the prince of Wales: 'God knows! where the young lady we want is to be found! Good looks, health, education, character, intellect and a good disposition we want; great rank and riches we do not', Victoria told her daughter (*Dearest Child*, 223). Eventually they settled on Alexandra of Denmark, although an alliance with Denmark was unfavourably regarded in Prussia. Victoria's family thus began the expansion which placed her direct descendants on ten European thrones and in dozens of other royal houses.

Victoria's and Albert's court

Court life under Victoria and Albert also took on a decidedly domestic and rather dull tone. Ceremonial was performed punctiliously when required, but with little enjoyment, for example at state openings of parliament and at levees and drawing-rooms, where the queen received the bows and curtseys of men and women wishing to be admitted to high society. Balls and concerts were held at Buckingham Palace, and the queen frequently attended the theatre and especially the opera, for which she retained her early love. She also enjoyed visits to Astley's circus, and the American showman Phineas T. Barnum was invited to bring the diminutive 'General' Tom Thumb to the palace three times in 1844. Such diversions were a welcome relief for courtiers, who were otherwise condemned to weeks of inactivity, literally 'in waiting' for the queen to require their services. Evenings could hang very heavy. A maid of honour, Eleanor Stanley, wrote of the dullness of the hours after dinner: the queen sat at one table with her ladies-in-waiting and female visitors, making conversation, and the maids of honour sat at another working at embroidery, while the prince remained in another room talking with the men for some time. He and 'one or two big-wigs' would then join the queen until she retired at 10.30, whereupon 'the other gentlemen make a rush from the whist-table or from the other room, and we gladly bundle up our work, and all is over' (Erskine, 176).

For visiting potentates a more ceremonial and formal programme of entertainments was devised, and courtiers were kept busy looking after their visiting counterparts. But Victoria's court was never glamorous and seldom sparkling. The queen was no fashion plate: the huge crinolines and poke bonnets of the 1840s and 1850s flattered few of their wearers, any more than the lurid colours they often chose. Victoria's dress sense was often the despair of the more fashion-conscious of her ladies and her dressers, especially when odious comparisons could be made between the queen and more elegant women. On the visit to France in 1843 Lady Canning was 'very much distressed to see our Queen appear in scarlet china crape [sic]' (V. Surtees, *Charlotte Canning*, 1975, 99); Victoria did not hesitate to wear it again, however, to receive Grand Duke Michael of Russia later in the year. Her shyness discouraged easy sociability, and conversation was often stilted because she would not initiate subjects about which she was ignorant.

Nothing contributed so much to the staid tenor of life at court as the regularity of court mourning. Victorian etiquette on mourning practices was rigorously prescriptive, and the correct degree of gloom for the passing of each of Victoria's and Albert's relations was observed, from complete black with no visitors or public appearances for three months for close relatives, to a day or two in 'slight mourning' for more distant connections. In 1852 the queen observed that she had been in mourning for nine months in every year for three or four years, and that since her marriage she had lost ten uncles and aunts. A lady-in-waiting was sorely tempted to ask 'And pray, Madam, how many more have you to lose?' (Erskine, 205). The toll of compulsory grief mounted through the 1850s: the duke of Wellington's death in 1852 was the cause of national mourning, while the court marked (among others) the deaths of Victoria's aunt the queen of Belgium in 1850, her uncle the king of Hanover in 1851, her half-brother Prince Charles of Leiningen in 1856, her cousin the duchess of Nemours (from complications after childbirth) in 1857, and the prince consort's stepmother in 1860. This was mere preparation for the mourning that was to come.

The year of desolation, 1861

The year 1861 began with a death in the family. The aged King Frederick William of Prussia died on 1 January, making Vicky and Fritz crown prince and princess of Prussia. In February Victoria and Albert celebrated their twenty-first wedding anniversary, 'a day which had brought us, and I may say the *world* at *large*, such incalculable blessings!' (*Letters*, 1st ser., 3.433). Then on 16 March the duchess of Kent died and Victoria suffered a nervous breakdown. Her relationship with the duchess, so tense during her teenage years, had been repaired by Albert, who had a firm idea of the appropriate relationship between a mother and daughter, and in old age the duchess had become beloved. Moreover, Victoria knew herself to be isolated by her position, and her mother was one of the few people with whom she could be open. Rumours about the queen's mental health flew about the courts of Europe, and it was with some difficulty that Albert brought her back into her public role to meet the king of Sweden in August.

Later in August the royal couple visited Ireland, the expedition planned to coincide with Bertie's military training at the Curragh. Still dwelling on her mother's death, Victoria set off with Albert in September for Balmoral, where Albert had planned several of the big expeditions they so enjoyed in the highlands. At the end of October they returned to Windsor, where they were confronted with news of the deaths in rapid succession of two of the sons of one of their Coburg cousins, Pedro V of Portugal and his brother Ferdinand, and then a report from the hand of the watchful Stockmar that the prince of Wales had been involved in an affair with an 'actress', Nelly Clifden. Victoria and Albert were horrified, not least because negotiations were in train for the prince's marriage to Princess Alexandra of Denmark. Albert's health, which had been poor for some years (modern diagnosis suggests he had cancer of the stomach or bowel), deteriorated rapidly. He had been suffering from a cold which he could not shake off. Victoria, wrapped up in her own misery, did not take Albert's condition seriously, and on 9 December she was finding her husband's illness 'tiresome': 'I need not tell you *what* a trial it is to me' (*Letters*, 1st ser., 3.470–71). On 11 December she was still feeling more for the difficulty of her own position while Albert was out of action, until the first public bulletins about his health were issued, when the full seriousness of his condition—believed to be typhoid fever—burst upon her. After three days of failing hopes Albert died on 14 December surrounded by his family, Victoria kneeling at his side and holding his hand.

The devastation Albert's death caused in his widow is the strongest evidence of his part in forming her character. That she loved him went without saying; but the dependence he had created in her left her unprotected and helpless at his death. Her prostration was total. In accordance with custom and her own preferences and feelings, Victoria plunged into deep mourning. The court was swathed in black clothing and crepe, and henceforth the thousands of letters from Victoria's pen were written on paper edged up to half an inch deep in black (leaving little space for the queen's angular handwriting), in black-trimmed envelopes, and sealed with black wax. It was customary also for the recently widowed to avoid public appearances, an embargo Victoria embraced with gloomy enthusiasm. To most of her subjects the queen's grief and her withdrawal from public and social life were natural, reasonable, and proper. It was only when her mourning exceeded the traditional period (which decreed one year of full mourning for a husband, followed by a second year of half-mourning and a lifetime of black gowns and white caps) that the disquiet already felt by the political élite became more widespread.

Victoria committed herself to Albert's memory: '*his* wishes—*his* plans—about everything, *his* views about *every* thing are to be *my law*! And no *human power* will make me swerve from *what he* decided and wished' (*Letters*, 1st ser., 3.606). The public initially sympathized. Statues were erected by public subscription in some twenty-five cities; hospitals, infirmaries, and museums were given his name;

and national memorials to the prince consort were built in London, Edinburgh, Dublin, and Tenby. Victoria responded by leaving her seclusion to appear in public and open several of the memorials. Her own memorials to Albert included Ludwig Gruner's and A. J. Humbert's Romanesque mausoleum at Frogmore, where Albert's remains were eventually interred, and the remodelling of the Wolsey chapel in St George's Chapel, Windsor, by G. G. Scott as the Albert memorial chapel. At Balmoral Victoria raised a cairn to his memory and erected a huge statue of him, and sculptors, painters, and photographers were kept busy with her commissions for likenesses of her lost husband. She commissioned Theodore Martin to write her husband's life in five volumes; she prepared the materials for *The Early Years of HRH the Prince Consort* (1867), which appeared over the name of her equerry, General Charles Grey; the clerk to the privy council, Arthur Helps, was selected to edit a volume of the prince's speeches. Helps was also called on by the queen to edit and introduce *Leaves from a Journal of our Life in the Highlands* (1868), which Victoria published as a tribute to Albert and as a substitute for public appearances.

Victoria's grief was genuine, fuelled by the feeling that she, like the public, had been insufficiently grateful for Albert during his lifetime, and she kept it stoked by creating images not only of the lost beloved, but also of her own sorrow: she seldom showed herself to anyone outside her family circle and circumscribed household, but by having her image captured as she gazed lovingly at a bust of Albert, surrounded by her younger children, she constantly viewed herself as a tragic heroine. Albert's image was everywhere about her: a photograph of him on his deathbed hung over his pillow in every bed the queen slept in.

Victoria's mourning caused an almost complete cessation of her public appearances. She resumed her day-to-day duties of reading dispatches, and her interest in foreign affairs soon had her again involved, making inimitable marginal comments on Foreign Office and Colonial Office papers. But she was unwilling for a time personally to receive ministers, who were to communicate with her through General Charles Grey or Princess Alice. When the privy council met, the queen sat in one room, the councillors in another, with Arthur Helps, the secretary to the council, acting as intermediary. Her workload was reduced by an act passed in March 1862 relieving her of triple-signing all army commissions (though she later resumed the practice). The queen's gloomy behaviour at the prince of Wales's marriage to Princess Alexandra of Denmark in March 1863 attracted unfavourable comment: she did not attend the wedding breakfast, and watched the ceremony from a secluded vantage point, in unrelieved black. It was a nice distinction between Benjamin Disraeli's view—that 'the presence of the imperial and widowed mother in her Gothic pavilion, watching everything with intense interest, seeing everything, though herself unseen, was deeply dramatic and even affecting' (Monypenny and Buckle, 4.397)—and the more general sense that the queen had been something of a wet blanket.

Royal opening of parliament had been willingly suspended in 1862, but by 1864 its absence was criticized, and not merely by the marginal or even radical press. On 1 April 1864

The Times's leader—the choice of date allowing for a licence of comment otherwise impossible—constituted a sustained sermon to the queen on her failure to do her public duty, and feigned to assume her imminent return to public life. On 6 April the queen herself wrote to the paper, with ill-concealed anonymity, to deny that she was 'about to resume the place in society which she occupied before her great affliction'. With a lead from *The Times*, other papers followed. In 1866, seeking a dowry for the marriage of her third daughter, Princess Helena, Victoria opened parliament, but avoided other public appearances, such as royal levees and drawing-rooms, which were held on her behalf by the prince and princess of Wales. In general, however, she refused to let the prince come forward as an alternative; she both blamed him for indolence, and opposed his emergence as a replacement for herself.

The madness of Queen Victoria?

Widowhood badly affected Victoria's character. Without Albert to urge self-control she gave in completely to her grief; her physical and mental health suffered, and her doctor Sir William Jenner provided medical authority for her incapacity to undertake public appearances. Nobody except Albert had ever had any power to make the queen do anything she found uncongenial; now, with the excuse of her great sorrow and her fragile health, her family and household spoke of 'the extreme difficulty there was in managing her or in the slightest degree contradicting her' (Kennedy, 189). Only the firmly held belief that she too would die soon and be reunited with Albert helped Victoria through the first years of her widowhood. Her convictions that the prince of Wales (whom she held responsible for Albert's death) was unfit for the throne and that monarchy was a sacred obligation prohibited abdication. As a result Victoria became profoundly selfish and self-centred, and her native stubbornness was given full play. Her world had revolved around Albert; now it would revolve around herself.

Beneath all the discussions about the queen's mourning were worries about madness. King George III had, after all, been her grandfather. His long illness was (probably wrongly) considered to have been insanity, and the behaviour of his sons, especially George IV, was widely viewed as (at best) eccentric. Fears of hereditary madness, of bad blood, dominated the Victorian imagination; moreover, women who transgressed the bounds of 'normal' femininity were liable to be labelled mad by a patriarchal establishment with an interest in maintaining the sexual status quo. Baron Stockmar had warned Albert of the possible instability of his wife, and successfully urged on him the need to contain Victoria's passionate temperament. Doctors too kept a constant vigil over Victoria's mental health, their prognostications of disaster given revived force by her regular postnatal depressions. After 1861 rumours of the queen's madness flourished, encouraged by her seclusion, and gossip about her state of mind filled the letters of concerned politicians. Well into the 1870s Lord Derby was commenting on her increasing peculiarities and supposing 'that she will be what her predecessors since George III inclusive have been, if her life extends to old age' (*Derby Diaries, 1869–1878*, ed. J. Vincent, 1994, 179). Fears of triggering outright madness contributed to the caution with which everyone approached the queen in the 1860s, and to their reluctance to contradict or thwart her. Suggestions of insanity were also a means of containing the perceived dangers of a woman on the throne who was still young but no longer under the appropriate control of a husband; they notably tailed off after the queen passed the menopause. Victoria could be temperamental, passionate, self-willed, opinionated, proud, selfish, obstinate, stubborn, and difficult, but she was not mad. Even after 1861, at the depths of her nervous prostration, she was simply very sad.

Mrs Brown

Victoria's sense of isolation after Albert's death was not easily alleviated. She had always enjoyed male company, but the proprieties restricted her as a widow to the society of women. Her unmarried daughters were too young to provide her daily support, and although she clung tenaciously to some of her female household, especially the duchesses of Suther-land and Atholl, Lady Ely, and Lady Augusta Bruce, in their company she could never bring herself to forget that she was the queen and they her subjects. Parliament (which feared placing an adviser about the queen who was not accountable to the ministry) was unwilling to concede that the queen needed a private secretary until 1867, when Charles Grey, formerly Albert's private secretary, was appointed. He gener-ally retained the queen's confidence despite making it clear, in his bluff way, that he thought her grief exaggerated.

In this desolate situation the royal servant, John Brown (1826–1883), who had become a permanent feature of the queen's daily life by 1865, seemed to Victoria sympathetic and understanding. He had been a regular attendant on the royal couple in the highlands and hence had Albert's seal of approval. Brown's domineering approach to the queen (unthinkable and unacceptable to her courtiers and family) was unique, being made possible by his lowly social position. No minister or secretary could say to her 'Hoots, then wumman. Can ye no hold yerr head up?' (Longford, 325). The exact degree of intimacy between the queen and John Brown cannot now be known (there is no evidence of marriage, despite many rumours and press reports), but Brown certainly became for a time the chief focus of the queen's emotional life, thereby helping to wean her from grief for her dead husband. Brown was especially useful to her during the late 1860s and early 1870s, but he remained her chief personal attendant until his death in 1883. The queen's grief on this occasion was unconfined, and she erected a large obelisk at Balmoral and a granite seat at Osborne to his memory.

In 1884, using his diaries, the queen wrote a memoir of Brown intended for private circulation. As Sir Henry Ponsonby (who had become her private secretary in 1870) at once saw, the document could not but be of sensational interest. He persuaded the queen to delay printing the memoir, and, according to his son and biographer, 'the papers were destroyed' (Ponsonby, 147). The destruction (if indeed it took place) was perhaps in the long run misguided: it has been taken by the prurient as evidence of an affair between the queen and Brown that her courtiers and family were anxious to hush up, whereas the mere fact of its being written tends to support the innocence of the relationship, for Victoria would never have publicized an illicit affair. When the queen published *More Leaves from a Journal of a*

Life in the Highlands (1884), she gave it a fulsome dedication to Brown (*Leaves* had been dedicated to Albert), with a conclusion specifically to his memory, remarking that 'he is daily, nay hourly, missed by me, whose lifelong gratitude he won by his constant care, attention, and devotion'.

Ending seclusion

Family affairs, affairs of state, 1861–1868

Victoria was soon drawn back to foreign affairs through the letters of her daughter Vicky: now crown princess of Germany, Vicky was an impotent witness to Bismarck's policy of uniting Germany through 'blood and iron'. With Albert's dearest hopes and plans for a liberal Germany unravelling fast, the queen had to acknowledge that her initial vow to follow his wishes and policy in everything was impossible to fulfil: by 1880 the world he had known had been completely transformed, and Victoria was wise enough to know he would not have tolerated many of the inevitable changes, 'which might have done him harm' (*Darling Child*, 239). The marriage of Princess Alice to Louis of Hesse in July 1862—'more like a funeral than a wedding', Victoria reported approvingly (ibid., 2.85)—took away the daughter on whom she had leant most after Albert's death, and a dispute arose between them in 1866, when Alice opposed the marriage of Princess Helena to Christian of Schleswig-Holstein-Augustenburg. That marriage also caused some ill feeling with the prince and princess of Wales, for it was arranged in the aftermath of the Prussian-Danish War, over Schleswig-Holstein. The Danish-born princess of Wales could seldom be brought to politeness to Prussians, which added to tensions in the family, and persuaded the queen to sanction the marriage in 1871 of Princess Louise to a commoner, the marquess of Lorne, heir to the dukedom of Argyll: 'Times have changed', she told the prince of Wales. '[G]reat foreign alliances are looked on as causes of trouble and anxiety, and are of no good' (*Letters*, 2nd ser., 1.632). It was the closest she came to criticizing Albert.

The death of Lord Palmerston in October 1865 forced Victoria to take a more active part in domestic politics. For the first time since 1840 she faced an important polit- ical interview alone, on the formation of the new ministry. She turned to Lord Russell to continue the administra- tion; 'strange, but these politicians never refuse' was King Leopold's cynical observation (*Letters*, 2nd ser., 1.281). It was one of the old campaigner's last comments; he died on 10 December, leaving Victoria to mourn one 'who has ever been to me as a Father' (ibid., 1.287). In 1866, with war brewing between Prussia and Austria, Victoria wrote to Lord Derby to hope that he would raise 'no violent or factious opposition' (ibid., 1.330) to parliamentary reform which, under Russell, was once more a live issue. She attempted to keep Russell's ministry in office when it was defeated on its Reform Bill in June 1866, by appealing to its duty to maintain stability in the face of continental war, but to no avail. Derby formed the new government with Benjamin Disraeli as chancellor of the exchequer; Victoria found him 'amiable and clever, but ... a strange man' (ibid., 1.379).

Disraeli succeeded Derby as prime minister in February 1868 and Victoria rapidly fell under his charm: 'he has always behaved extremely well to me, and has all the right feelings for a Minister towards the Sovereign', she told Vicky. He was, moreover, 'full of poetry, romance and chivalry' (*Your Dear Letter*, 176), qualities that had been sadly lacking in the queen's life in recent years. He enchanted the queen with references to her experience, wisdom, and abilities, declaring 'It will be his delight and duty to render the transaction of affairs as easy to your Majesty, as possible', and asking her guidance in 'the great affairs of state' (*Letters*, 2nd ser., 1.505). This was a very different sort of minister from any she had had before. Only Peel and Aberdeen had shown such 'care for my personal affairs or that respect and deference for me' (*Your Dear Letter*, 208), and they had never called her wise or sought her guidance. Disraeli's failure at the polls in November 1868 brought their promising relationship to a temporary end. Albert had thought Disraeli an adventurer, an unprincipled rogue. He had given his seal of approval instead to William Ewart Gladstone, the disciple of Peel and Aberdeen, but his widow did not renew it.

The first Gladstone ministry

Victoria had encountered Gladstone regularly over the preceding twenty years; under Albert's guidance she admired his religious earnestness and his cleverness. Without Albert these virtues overbalanced into their opposites: she suspected him of 'humbug' (hypocrisy), and his cold intellectualism both intimidated and repelled her. Gladstone, like Albert, had a theoretical mind. Victoria's sharp intelligence was at its best with the concrete. Gladstone had twice resigned from government (in 1845 and again in 1855); on neither occasion had he been in disagreement with his colleagues, and on both occasions his explanation left the queen bewildered. Gladstone was not quite 'safe', a little 'strange'. Nor did his personal manner endear him to Victoria. He was a committed monarchist, with an almost religious reverence for the role of the queen, but he could never forget he was dealing with his sovereign, and while treating her as an intelligent mind, he never managed to absorb the advice of his wife, to treat her also as a woman. 'I cannot find him very agreeable, and he talks so very much', Victoria grumbled (*Your Dear Letter*, 248). One of the few things that united them was opposition to the growing movement for women's suffrage. Responding in 1870 to an anti-feminist pamphlet which Gladstone had forwarded to her, Victoria declared 'the strongest aversion for the *socalled & most erroneous* "Rights of Woman" ' (P. Guedalla, ed., *The Queen and Mr Gladstone*, 1933, 1.221).

Gladstone's foremost aim in his first ministry was, as is well known, 'to pacify Ireland'. His second objective was to bring the queen out of her seclusion and to restore her place at the ceremonial head of government. Concerned about the queen's absence from public view, he had frequently discussed the subject with his closest contact at court, Harriet, duchess of Sutherland, mistress of the robes under successive whig ministries from 1837. The slow rise of a popular republican movement gained pace in the late 1860s (coupled with violent acts and threats from Irish Fenians), and Gladstone was concerned above all that the queen should not give it extra fuel by her invisibility. Those who did not have to deal with her on a regular basis sometimes thought his concern exaggerated. Lord Kimberley, for example, regretted her 'somewhat selfish seclusion', but considered that 'the nation will forgive a great deal in a woman, and besides she has many admirable qualities which go far to redeem some weaknesses' (E. Drus, ed., *A Journal of Events during the Gladstone Ministry, 1868–1874*, 1958, 26). But Gladstone's was not the only voice urging the queen to resume her public role, or warning of potential dangers if she did not. Her children—particularly the prince of Wales, who had a vested interest—periodically plucked up courage to hint that her actions were not best calculated to protect and enhance her throne; King Leopold had reminded her in 1864 that the British needed to see their rulers; a few of her courtiers, including Lady Augusta Stanley and the dean of Windsor, gently encouraged her to lessen her mourning.

Victoria felt bullied, beleaguered, and besieged. Everyone, she felt, was against her, no one understood—or cared about—her feelings and needs; she maintained, with some justification, that she worked extremely hard for the country, studying the huge quantities of official papers sent to her, corresponding with her ministers and attempting to keep national (rather than merely party) interests in their minds, continuing an extensive international correspondence with other courts in the effort to keep the peace, trying, above all, to live up to the standards Albert had set. What she would not do was that on which her ministers—Gladstone in particular, it seemed—set the greatest store. She would not appear in public to be stared at by curious crowds, she would not put off her mourning to wear the official regalia of her position, and she would not endure unnecessary ceremonial.

Gladstone's attempts to persuade the queen to reverse her policy failed almost completely for three years, and in the process he equally completely alienated her. His policies, too, Victoria found uncongenial, especially those on the army and Ireland. 'There is so little true feeling of loyalty in many of these clever radicals', she wrote. 'They would alter everything without being able to put better things in their place' (*Your Dear Letter*, 236). She was persuaded to abolish the purchase of army commissions by royal warrant, despite the opposition of her cousin the commander-in-chief, the duke of Cambridge: if nothing else, she was glad to exercise prerogative powers over the issue. The disestablishment of the Church of Ireland in 1869 touched on her prerogative as head of the Anglican church, and it was partly displeasure at the proposal which led her to decline to open parliament in person that year. Gladstone's plan to reform both the Irish Office and the frivolous habits of the prince of Wales by sending him to Dublin as viceroy met scornful rejection from the queen whenever the subject was raised.

Victoria rigorously shut the prince of Wales out from involvement in her political business. Instead, he and the princess of Wales threw themselves into the pleasure-loving world of aristocratic society, the very world against which Albert had sought to inoculate his family, and of which Victoria disapproved: 'The higher classes—especially the aristocracy ... —are so frivolous, pleasure-seeking, heartless, selfish, immoral and gambling that it makes one think ... of the days before the French Revolution', she wrote

Her son's excesses contributed to the growing anti-monarchical sentiment in British politics. When, in 1870, he was exposed as a licentious playboy during the notorious Mordaunt divorce case, the queen was isolated at Windsor, herself the subject of rumour and scandal at the height of the Brown affair.

Public criticism of the monarchy mounted through 1871, with the publication of a pamphlet, *What does she do with it?*, subjecting the queen's finances to scrutiny, and a speech by Sir Charles Dilke at Newcastle in November advocating a republican alternative. At the end of November the queen was recovering from several months' extreme ill health—her symptoms this time were physical, with abscesses on her arm, gout, and rheumatic pains and fever—when she received news that the prince of Wales had typhoid fever. His illness reached a crisis on the anniversary of the prince consort's death and, in the national rejoicing at his recovery, the republican moment was lost. Gladstone urged the value of a service of thanksgiving at St Paul's Cathedral; Victoria resisted energetically, but for once her prime minister prevailed, and on 27 February 1872 the queen drove in state through London, greeted by 'wonderful enthusiasm and astounding affectionate loyalty' (*Letters*, 2nd ser., 2.194). Two days later Arthur O'Connor thrust a pistol at the queen as she was returning to Buckingham Palace after a drive in her carriage but was seized by the faithful Brown before he could make his demand for the release of Fenian prisoners. Public sympathy for her was immense.

The thanksgiving of 1872 was a turning point for the monarchy, setting a precedent for the huge ceremonial functions of later years, and for Victoria herself, who was surprised and affected by the enthusiasm of her reception and gradually allowed herself to shed some of the adjuncts of misery which she had wrapped around herself. She still resisted opening parliament, and refused to alter her rigid schedule of visits to Scotland and the Isle of Wight, but she did agree to receive the shah of Persia in 1873 on a state visit and went so far as to wear the koh-i-noor diamond in brooch form to greet him. Public criticism ended almost overnight. From the nadir of 1871 Victoria's popularity increased year on year before reaching a virtual apotheosis in the jubilee years of 1887 and 1897.

Crown imperial: Dizzy and the Faery

By the end of Gladstone's first ministry (1874) Victoria had finally discovered a political confidence which the long years of tutelage under Albert had subjugated and which, with a congenial prime minister, she was keen to bring into action. Her longevity, coupled with an accurate and detailed memory, became her principal political assets, which increased with time. She was the one constant feature of the nineteenth-century political scene, and this gave her voice much of its authority.

The success of the Conservatives at the polls in February 1874 brought Disraeli back into office, to the queen's delight. His wife having died in 1872, he was now more welcome than ever. On kissing hands as prime minister he said, 'I plight my troth to the kindest of *Mistresses*!' (*Letters*, 2nd ser., 2.322). It was the true beginning of a mutually beneficial partnership, which contained elements of both romance and farce. He frankly admitted to his use of flattery and recommended that for a royal audience 'you should lay it on with a trowel' (Longford, 401). Unlike Gladstone, Disraeli never forgot that he was addressing a woman as well as his sovereign; she, by turns, enjoyed the chivalric flirtation which perhaps more closely resembled her relationship with Melbourne than that with any man since her marriage. To Albert she had always been his 'gutes Frauchen' ('good little wife'), or 'beloved child'. He would never have thought of the fanciful name Disraeli bestowed on the queen, 'The Faery'; he would never have said, as Disraeli did, that *whatever I wished should be done*, whatever his difficulties might be' (*Letters*, 2nd ser., 2.321). If there was something fantastical, even ridiculous, about a man of seventy with dyed black ringlets addressing a short, stout woman of over fifty in the language of Spenser's *Faerie Queene*, it was in itself a harmless enough amusement. The negative side of Disraeli's flowery compliments was that the queen's sense of her powers moved out of step with contemporary thinking on the monarch's role in the constitution: Lord Derby, whose hostility to the queen was veiled but not hidden, cautioned his chief against 'encouraging her in too large ideas of her personal power, and too great indifference to what the public expects' (Blake, 548). Disraeli too occasionally reminded the queen of the realities of their positions: 'Were he your Majesty's Grand Vizier, instead of your Majesty's Prime Minister, he should be content to pass his remaining years in accomplishing everything your Majesty wished; but, alas! it is not so' (*Letters*, 2nd ser., 2.385).

Victoria's alliance with Disraeli rested on more than personal attraction, however. In the changed circumstances of the European political scene of the late 1860s and 1870s, in which Bismarck's united Germany loomed large and the general European peace looked increasingly fragile, she was desperately concerned to maintain British prestige and power. She had witnessed the effects of war in the 1850s, and throughout the 1860s her family was shaken by the effects of Bismarck's wars, which placed her children on different sides of the conflicts. War, she concluded, was terrible; more terrible, however, would be the effect of a general European belief that Britain would not engage in warfare. Russia was her particular bugbear, despite cordial personal relations with the tsar and his family. She shared Disraeli's view that Russia posed a serious threat to British interests in India, and that Russian expansion into the Mediterranean, via a collapsing Turkey, was to be prevented at all costs. 'I have but one object', she wrote in 1877, 'the honour and dignity of this country' (*Darling Child*, 251). Disraeli's brand of Conservatism, with its forward foreign policy, seemed to her to share her perspective.

Disraeli, above all, had the measure of how to manage the queen: 'I never deny; I never contradict; I sometimes forget' (Longford, 403). Victoria rewarded his tact by opening parliament in person three times during his ministry (in 1876, 1877, and 1880), giving a public mark of approval to her prime minister. If Disraeli expected his vows of personal devotion and service to be understood strictly rhetorically, however, he was soon disabused. The queen had become increasingly concerned in the early 1870s at the rise of the ritualist party within the Church of England and its 'Romanising tendencies' (*Letters*, 2nd ser., 2.290). She was herself, by necessity and inclination, 'Protestant to the very *heart's core*' (ibid., 2.302): her personal preference was for extremely simple services, and she argued for greater unity among the different protestant churches. (She took communion at a Presbyterian service at Crathie kirk for the first time on 3 November 1873, having previously held back from scruple as to her position at the head of the episcopalian church.) In 1873 she began to badger Gladstone to bring in legislation to outlaw ritualist practices in the Church of England, knowing him to be high-church and believing him to be a ritualist sympathizer, if not actually a secret Romanist. Disraeli was less able to withstand her onslaught, and the Public Worship Regulation Act of 1874 owed much to her pressure.

The Royal Titles Act of 1876 was also close to Victoria's heart, and caused Disraeli considerable political difficulties. Since 1858, when Britain assumed direct control of the territories formerly managed by the East India Company, the queen had been spoken of informally as the empress of India. Victoria was now delighted by Disraeli's proposal that 'empress of India' be added to her formal style, although she was keen to point out that it would make no difference to her style in Britain, believing the title was 'best understood in the East, but which Great Britain (which *is an Empire*) never has acknowledged to be higher than King or Queen' (*Letters*, 2nd ser., 2.450–51).

She denied it strongly, but the fact that the unified Germany now had an emperor (and her daughter would one day be empress) and that her second son, Alfred, had married into the Russian imperial family in 1873 also weighed with her, as issues of precedence and rank arose: the senior monarch

of Europe, she would not allow her family to be belittled as Albert had been by rank-conscious foreigners. She
found the outcry against the new title incomprehensible,
dismissing Liberal objections as mere party factionalism:
her relationship with Lord Granville (who had formerly
been the acceptable face of the Gladstonian administration)
never recovered from his publicly stated opposition. She was
proclaimed empress of India on 1 January 1877 at a spec-
tacular durbar at Delhi, stage-managed by the viceroy, Lord
Lytton, and the same day signed herself for the first time
'Victoria R & I' ('Victoria regina et imperatrix', Victoria,
queen and empress). It was intended that she should use
the new designation only in her dealings with India, but she
soon made it her usual style.

It was in Victoria's response to the crisis in the Balkans in the
later 1870s that Disraeli reaped as he had sown, as the queen
sought to drive him to an ever more interventionist policy.
Evading her private secretary, Henry Ponsonby (who had
succeeded Charles Grey in 1870), who was a whig and whom
she unjustly suspected of disloyalty to her prime minister,
she bombarded Disraeli with letters, telegrams, and memoranda. She initially sympathized with the Christians in the
Balkans in 1876 (the victims of the 'Bulgarian atrocities')
but, as the question increasingly focused on the fact that
it was the Russian rather than the British government that
acted to protect them, Victoria became passionately engaged
in keeping her government up to the mark in opposing
Russian action against Turkey. Between April 1877 and February 1878 she five times threatened abdication if Beaconsfield (as Disraeli became when ennobled in 1876) did not
hold firm, and she encouraged her prime minister to force

the resignations of Lord Carnarvon and Lord Derby, leaders of the conciliatory group in the cabinet. By treating policy as a game of flirtatious verbiage, Beaconsfield encouraged the queen in her enthusiasms, although in the long run all her frenetic activity had little impact on the course of events.

Outside Europe, Beaconsfield's active imperialism gave his sovereign two wars, the Anglo-Zulu War and the Second Anglo-Afghan War, and embroiled the country inextricably in imperial expansion. Prestige was no longer a purely European matter, and Victoria endorsed his policy enthusiastically, fully accepting that 'If *we* are to *maintain* our position as a *first-rate* Power—and of that *no one* ... can doubt, we must ... be *prepared* for *attacks* and *wars*, somewhere or *other*, CONTINUALLY' (*Letters*, 2nd ser., 3.37–8). It has been pointed out that 'there was not a single year in Queen Victoria's long reign in which somewhere in the world her soldiers were not fighting for her and for her empire' (B. Farwell, *Queen Victoria's Little Wars*, 1973, 1). With the European powers competing to acquire colonial empires, more and more of those conflicts and actions took place in Africa, and Victoria's interest in the colonies (which had been rather lukewarm until now) became intense. She supported Beaconsfield's policies publicly and privately, and sent a telegram of sympathy and encouragement to the commanding general in South Africa after the defeat of the British at the hands of the Zulu at Isandlwana in January 1879. Her commitment to the empire remained unshaken even after the death in battle of the prince imperial, son of the deposed Napoleon III, later in the same war, and the disastrous loss of the mission to

Afghanistan in September 1879. Victoria viewed her empire as benignly civilizing: 'the Native Sovereigns CANNOT maintain their authority ... It is not for aggrandisement, but to prevent war and bloodshed that we must do this [that is, take possession]', she told Beaconsfield (*Letters*, 2nd ser., 3.43).

When Beaconsfield asked for a dissolution of parliament in March 1880, Victoria hoped that 'the Government will do well in the elections' (*Beloved Mama*, 71); she did not delay her planned visit to Darmstadt for the confirmation of Alice's daughters and to Baden-Baden, where she received Beaconsfield's telegram announcing the defeat of his ministry: 'The Queen cannot deny she (Liberal as she has ever been, but never Radical or democratic) thinks it a great calamity for the country and the peace of Europe!' (*Letters*, 2nd ser., 3.73).

Victoria's dramatic transformation from the glumly dutiful, nearly invisible 'widow of Windsor' into this dynamically engaged, energetic interventionist owed much to her personal relationship with Disraeli, and also something to the experience of 1871–2. But more, perhaps, was owed to a radical shift within Victoria herself. Her personality had been re-formed by Albert after 1840 and it underwent a kind of disintegration after his death. By the 1870s Victoria's personality had reasserted itself, and characteristics that had been sublimated for almost thirty years reasserted themselves: the Victoria of 1837–41 was easily recognizable in the Victoria of 1876–86. The queen was sixty-one in 1880; she had now reigned alone for almost as long as her dual monarchy with Albert had lasted. The violence of her feelings on Gladstone's return to office and the continual struggles with him over the next fifteen years showed just how thin was the veneer of impartiality and self-control that Albert had placed over her natural inclinations after 1840.

Grandmother of Europe

7

The royal family

By relaxing her seclusion Victoria reduced one of the major sources of tension with her elder children. Not that all was plain sailing: the prince of Wales remained irredeemably frivolous and worldly (although his mother was now more willing to admit and praise his good qualities); Alfred (created duke of Edinburgh in 1866) was safely married to Grand Duchess Marie of Russia after some years of alarm, but he was indiscreet politically and the queen worried about his connections with his in-laws. Victoria's relationships with her married daughters also fluctuated, especially over their regular childbearing. Even with Vicky there were periodic coolnesses, sometimes over politics, but more often over her 'inconsiderate' habit of visiting the queen with a large suite of courtiers. The death of Princess Alice from diphtheria in 1878 on the anniversary of the prince consort's death was the first breach in the family circle (excepting a few tiny children, victims of the high infant mortality rate which even royalty could not escape); the queen mourned the 'precious child who stood by me and upheld me seventeen years ago' (*Beloved Mama*, 30), but was not prostrated as the crown princess feared.

As Victoria's youngest son, Leopold (created duke of Albany in 1881), grew up he resented the restrictions the queen placed around him: constantly anxious over his health, she attempted to keep him away from the social life of his brother and refused to allow him to take up a career. From 1876 she used him as an unofficial private secretary (part of her method of evading Ponsonby), and even gave him keys to the dispatch boxes, a privilege she denied her heir until much later. He was permitted to marry Princess Helen of Waldeck-Pyrmont in 1882—'such a risk and experiment', the queen thought (*Beloved Mama*, 111). His death in March 1884 from complications of the epilepsy and haemophilia which had restricted his life was 'an awful blow' (ibid., 162–3). Princess Beatrice, the youngest child, was brought up to be the daughter at home, the prop and mainstay of her mother. 'She is like a sunbeam in the house and also like a dove, an angel of peace who brings it wherever she goes and who is my greatest comfort', Victoria wrote (*Darling Child*, 290). Marriage was never to be mentioned in front of her, but in 1884 she met Prince Henry of Battenberg and fell in love. The queen was horrified at first, but was eventually induced to consent on condition that Beatrice and Henry (or Liko, as the family called him) should always live with her. Only Arthur, duke of Connaught (so created in 1874), always her favourite son, gave the queen unalloyed pleasure, making a successful career in the army and marrying the suitable Princess Louise of Prussia in 1878.

The inevitable result of the marriages of all Victoria's offspring was the proliferation of grandchildren (thirty-four survived childhood) and, before long, great-grandchildren: Victoria was a grandmother at thirty-nine and a great-grandmother at sixty. Only Princess Louise remained childless, for even Leopold had fathered two children in the two years of his marriage, his son being born posthumously. Victoria still found babies a bore, and the size of her family was a continual source of grumbling: 'when they come at the rate of three a year it becomes a cause of mere anxiety for my own children and of no great interest', she told the crown princess, who had just produced her fourth daughter and eighth child (*Darling Child*, 40). Sons in particular were a problem—'I think many Princes a great misfortune—for they are in one another's and almost everybody's way' (ibid.). But as they put aside babyhood, she interested herself minutely in the details of their upbringing and in the arrangement of their marriages. The five surviving motherless Hesse children spent a lot of time in Britain with their grandmother, while Beatrice's four children grew up in the household of 'Grandmamma Queen'. The grandchild who consumed most of Victoria's attention was not the heir presumptive to her own throne, the prince of Wales's eldest son, Albert Victor (who should perhaps have worried her more; his early death in 1892 saved Britain the embarrassment of a barely literate monarch implicated in numerous carefully hushed-up scandals), or his brother George, later King George V. Rather, it was Vicky's eldest son, William, who from an early age was taught by his paternal grandfather to despise his parents and particularly his British mother: endless concern flowed between the two Victorias about the future German Kaiser, who idolized his

Court and household

Victoria's court never went out of mourning after 1861; her
ladies-in-waiting (many of whom were themselves widows)
joined the queen in perpetual black silk, but the younger
maids of honour wore white, grey, mauve, or purple (except
when another death put them back into black). Equally
immutable was the queen's routine: Christmas and the new
year were spent at Osborne, then the early part of the year
was spent at Windsor, with a few days in London. She
went to Balmoral in time for her birthday in May, then
returned to Windsor in June, before spending most of July
and August at Osborne. Late in August she would go back
to Balmoral; she would remain there until November, when
she returned to Windsor, before leaving for Osborne as soon
as the anniversary of the prince consort's death had passed.
Little was allowed to interfere with this regime, a source of
constant disquiet to her ministers. Despite improved travel
facilities and the invention of the telegraph, the queen in
Scotland was inconveniently inaccessible, especially after
1868, when she built a villa, the Glassalt Shiel, at the end
of Loch Muick, to which she regularly retreated. Inevitably,
with so many people kept in close confinement jostling (in
however restrained a fashion) for the ear of the queen, the
court itself became a hotbed of petty feuds, trivial disagree-
ments blown up into full-scale 'rows', misunderstandings
transformed into ill feeling. The all-pervasive influence of
John Brown did not help; nor did the queen's habit of indi-
rect communication. Rather than confront people directly,

she preferred to make her feelings known through little notes or through intermediaries; when the messenger was Brown or some other lesser mortal and the recipient one of her children, tempers often flared.

After Brown's death in 1883 the atmosphere lightened somewhat. The marriage of Princess Beatrice brought a cheerful, easy-going masculine presence into the queen's family, and Victoria permitted the gloom to be lifted by a little sedate liveliness: amateur theatricals enlivened the court periodically, and the tableaux vivants of which the Victorians were so fond were produced. The queen never went to a theatre after 1861, but in 1881 the prince of Wales persuaded her to attend a command performance of F. C. Burnand's *The Colonel* at his highland residence Abergeldie Castle. The experiment was a success, and in 1887 Victoria had the Kendals brought to Osborne to perform; thereafter command performances at Balmoral and Windsor enabled the queen to see the great performers of the day, from Henry Irving and Ellen Terry to Eleanora Duse and Sarah Bernhardt (who performed for the queen during a visit to Cimiez in 1897).

In the second half of her reign Victoria's court attracted little public attention. Other than her private secretary, Ponsonby (a model of discretion), her principal courtiers were elderly women: pre-eminent among the ladies-in-waiting were Jane, marchioness of Ely; Jane, Lady Churchill; and Anne, duchess of Atholl. Harriet Phipps (daughter of her keeper of the privy purse, Sir Charles Phipps) and Horatia Stopford were originally maids of honour, but in time became permanent bedchamber women. They acted as personal secretaries and assistants to the queen, who bullied them unmercifully: they read to her and dealt with her private and personal correspondence. In the 1890s they were joined by Marie Mallet. Victoria had always valued her physicians: Sir William Jenner was consulted on matters beyond mere health, and in 1881 she appointed James Reid, a young Scottish doctor, as her personal physician. In the 1890s (after Henry of Battenberg's death) Reid in some measure took the place Brown had occupied, both in the queen's esteem and in managing the household. But unlike Brown, Reid was almost universally popular: he could smooth over difficulties with a jest.

Victoria rampant: the second Gladstone ministry

From the 1870s the queen's court almost exclusively comprised Conservatives and Unionists. Sir Henry Ponsonby was the single exception, and he alone of the courtiers recognized the dangers of the queen's being surrounded by associates of a uniform political stripe, especially when that stripe belonged to the opposition. 'Incessant sneers or conversation against a policy always damages', he remarked (Ponsonby, 154), concluding that Sir Robert Peel had been right to insist on changing the ladies of the household with the ministry. 'Perhaps', he added, 'now it does not really matter whether the Queen dislikes them [her ministers] or not' (ibid.). Gladstone's second ministry put that question to the test.

Victoria had greeted Gladstone's electoral defeat in 1874 with ill-concealed glee. She quoted Palmerston's assessment that Gladstone was 'a very dangerous man', and went on to catalogue his failings: 'so very arrogant, tyrannical and obstinate, with no knowledge of the world or human nature . . . a fanatic in religion . . . and much want of *égard* towards my feelings . . . make him a very dangerous and unsatisfactory Premier' (*Darling Child*, 130). His retirement as leader of the Liberal Party in 1875 raised her hopes that she would not have to deal with him again, but she was sadly disappointed, for the 'Bulgarian atrocities' brought him out of retirement in 1876. In September 1876 Victoria found his campaign 'incomprehensible', and considered him 'most mischievous—though I believe unintentionally so' (ibid., 222). Ten days later the qualifier had gone: he was 'most reprehensible and mischievous', deliberately making the government's task more difficult (ibid., 223). In February 1877 he was 'that half madman Mr Gladstone' (ibid., 242), and by May 'that madman Gladstone' (ibid., 251). Her hope that the tories would return from the polls in 1880 'stronger than ever' was misplaced. Furious at what she considered the demagoguery of Gladstone's Midlothian campaigns of 1879–80 and anxious above all to exclude him from the premiership, she went to considerable lengths to find an alternative, inviting first Lord Hartington and then Lord Granville to form the administration. The effect of her intervention was to strengthen Gladstone's position, as the weakness of the potential alternative Liberal leaders was exposed.

The queen had boxed herself into a dangerous corner, for she faced at least several years of Liberal government with a large majority, having made her commitment to the policies of the Conservative Party transparent by her demeanour and her remarks to her courtiers. Mary Ponsonby, the wife of the queen's private secretary and herself a formidable intelligence, reflected in 1878 that 'Dizzy has worked the idea of personal government to its logical conclusion', an idea planted by Stockmar and Albert, who had 'kept the thing between bounds, but they established the superstition in the Queen's mind about her own prerogative', which could be exploited by an unscrupulous minister. She concluded that:

> If there comes a real collision between the Queen and the House of Commons...it is quite possible she would turn restive, *dorlotède* [coddled] as she has been by Dizzy's high sounding platitudes, and then her reign will end in a fiasco. (M. Ponsonby, ed., *Mary Ponsonby*, 1927, 144–5)

It was a perceptive analysis: Victoria was fortunate that Gladstone, and Lords Granville, and Rosebery—the chief ministers concerned—were careful to hide the full extent of her hostility even from the Liberal cabinet. Moreover, it was the Liberal Party, and especially its leadership, which was vital to the queen in the matter of royal finances, and she was fortunate that Gladstone did not use the issue to extract a quid pro quo.

The queen—always low-church in her opinions—approved of some Liberal measures, such as the Burials Bill (1880), which allowed dissenters to use Anglican graveyards, and the Deceased Wife's Sister Bill (1883); but on questions of foreign, defence, south African, and Irish policy there were constant confrontations and friction, especially when Beaconsfield's policy in the Near East was threatened. A row over the paragraph in the queen's speech in January 1881 on the evacuation of Kandahar in Afghanistan made a tetchy start. The queen disliked most aspects of the Liberal government's Irish legislation, and particularly its land legislation, on which she had an inside source: the father-in-law of her daughter Louise, the duke of Argyll, who resigned from the cabinet in March 1881 over the Irish Land Bill.

Argyll's resignation was followed in April 1881 by Beaconsfield's death. The queen had continued her correspondence with her former prime minister on political and personal matters after Beaconsfield went out of office, Victoria preferring to hear his account of proceedings in the House of Lords to that provided by her ministers. 'I look always to *you* for ultimate help', she assured him in September 1880 (*Letters*, 2nd ser., 3.143). The queen's various tributes to her former prime minister attracted much attention. (Beaconsfield on his deathbed remarked, when offered a royal visit, 'No, it is better not. She would only ask me to take a message to Albert' (Blake, 747).) These two events increased Victoria's political isolation, the second much more than the first, for Argyll differed sharply from her on Indian and Near Eastern policy, and, though the queen saw him as her last '*independent* and true friend' in the Gladstone cabinet, he was never quite the source of Liberal cabinet leaks for which she hoped. A rare moment of conciliation occurred in the autumn of 1884, when the queen encouraged a compromise between the Commons, which had passed a Representation of the People Bill, and the Lords, which declined to proceed with it without an accompanying measure of redistribution, which the government said would be its next legislative measure. The queen thought the Lords right, but feared the consequences of a popular movement against them, which might revive the republicanism of the early 1870s. How far the queen's mediation was significant is disputed, but her intentions were clear: 'I have worked very hard to try and bring about a meeting of the two sides in which I have succeeded so that they may try and come to an agreement upon these difficult questions of reform' (5 November 1884, *Beloved Mama*, 170–71).

Victoria was incensed by the Gladstone government's handling of the Sudanese question in 1883–5, when General Gordon met his death at Khartoum before Garnet Wolseley's relief expedition reached him: 'We were just too late as we always are—it is I, who have, as the Head of the Nation, to bear the humiliation'. She believed Gladstone 'will be forever branded with the blood of Gordon that heroic man' (*Beloved Mama*, 182–3), and she publicized her fury at the government with a rebuke unprecedented and unrepeated in the history of the British constitutional monarchy: she telegraphed *en clair* (that is, not in code, thus ensuring immediate leaks to the press) to Granville, Hartington, and Gladstone: 'These news from Khartoum are frightful, and to think that all this might have been prevented and many precious lives saved by earlier action is too frightful' (*Letters*, 2nd ser., 3.597). Popular though this view may have been, its public expression was scarcely in keeping with the queen's obligation to support her ministers, and contrasted markedly with Victoria's public affirmation of confidence in the authorities after the battle of Isandlwana in January 1879.

Home rule and Unionism

The Irish question and the relationship of Ireland to the other constituent parts of the United Kingdom were a central issue of Victoria's reign. It did not attract her early enthusiasm. Even so, encouraged by Albert, she visited the country more than her prime ministers, who went as such only twice: Russell in 1848, and Gladstone for a morning in 1880. The queen visited Dublin (creating the prince of Wales earl of Dublin) and Belfast in September 1849. She visited Dublin again in August–September 1851 and in September 1861, on this occasion venturing as far as Killarney. But these were visits which presupposed Ireland to be a place of danger. There was to be no Irish Balmoral, and after Albert's death the visits ceased until the very end of her reign, when, on her own initiative, she visited Dublin in April 1900. In the interim she refused all suggestions (chiefly, but not exclusively, proposals from Gladstone) that there be a royal residence and a regular royal presence in Ireland.

The queen, who was personally moved by the murder of Lord Frederick Cavendish in Dublin in May 1882, had no sympathy for those ministers who met the Land League of the early 1880s with anything other than coercion. She quickly and perceptively sensed the significance of the cabinet's change of direction in the spring of 1882. She felt she had been pressured by the cabinet into agreeing to the release of the Irish politician Charles Stewart Parnell in May 1882, and she thought Gladstone's policy of releasing prisoners disastrous, Joseph Chamberlain an 'evil genius', the home-rulers 'dreadful'. She complained to the prince of Wales about her 'dreadfully Radical Government which contains many thinly-veiled *Republicans*—and the way they have truckled to the Home Rulers—as well as the utter disregard of all my opinions which after 45 years of experience ought to be considered', and she blamed Hartington for failing to take office in 1880 and thus leaving her with 'this most dangerous man [Gladstone]' (*Letters*, 2nd ser., 3.298–9). She encouraged the prince to speak to Liberal ministers who might support her views: that she had to request her son to do this showed the extent of her alienation from her cabinet.

In the great political crisis of 1885–6, when Gladstone introduced a Government of Ireland Bill to provide for home rule together with a further Land Bill, and the Liberal Party split in consequence, Victoria was an enthusiastic protagonist on the Unionist side, and not a passive spectator as she had been when the tories split over free trade in 1846. The queen, predicting a Conservative defeat in the election of November 1885 and dreading the return of Gladstone, tried to prepare the ground for G. J. Goschen to lead a coalition. Victoria opened parliament on 21 January 1886, the last occasion on which she did so. When Lord Salisbury's government was defeated in the debate on the queen's speech, she refused to accept his resignation in 'an almost incoherent outpouring of protest and dismay' (G. Cecil, *Life of Robert, Marquis of Salisbury*, 3, 1931, 290). When Goschen declined the queen's commission, Ponsonby avoided a dangerous crisis by going immediately to Gladstone, though it was after midnight, and successfully gained the queen's objective of having Rosebery made foreign secretary. Throughout Gladstone's third government, which fell in June 1886 when the Home Rule Bill was defeated in the Commons, the queen sent Lord Salisbury copies of all Gladstone's important letters to her, and some of her replies to him (Longford, 485). Melbourne's legacy on this unconstitutional practice had cast a long shadow. The tories were thus exceptionally well placed to engineer the Liberal split which was Salisbury's chief objective during Gladstone's attempt to achieve an Irish constitutional settlement. She even went so far as to ask Salisbury, the leader of the opposition, to let her know if she should refuse the prime minister a dissolution, should he ask for it (as Gladstone did, following the defeat of his bill).

It is easy to characterize Victoria's position during this her most politically active decade as political partisanship, pure and simple. Undeniably, she lent all the support she could to Disraeli and to Lord Salisbury, and hindered as far as possible the radical agenda of Gladstone's successive ministries. The constitutional rights of the monarch, as expressed by Walter Bagehot in *The English Constitution* (a volume Victoria did not read and would not have approved if she had), to be consulted, to encourage, and to warn, were interpreted by the queen as the rights 'to instruct, to abuse, and to hector' (Matthew, 2.260). And yet Victoria did not see herself as partisan—which had been Albert's great lesson— or even as Conservative. She considered herself a liberal constitutional monarch; it was Gladstone who had abandoned liberalism for radicalism or even democracy, Gladstone who threatened the constitutional arrangements of the country, Gladstone who took issues of national significance, security, or prestige and made party-political capital out of them. Disraeli had persuaded her that she herself stood for the national interest; by making the monarchy an important element of tory democracy, he had allied his party with the queen. Now she was convinced that 'all moderate, loyal and *really patriotic* men, who have the safety and well-being of the Empire and Throne at heart, and who wish to save them from destruction' had a duty to 'rise above party and be true patriots!' (*Letters*, 2nd ser., 3.712–13). Her views were reinforced by her narrow reading of the press, for she relied on two Conservative papers, the *Morning Post* and the *St James's Gazette*. The queen was thus a proponent of the notions that Conservatism was not an ideology, that radicalism was incompatible with patriotism, and that her own views reflected, by definition, the national interest.

Salisbury, Rosebery, and the late Victorian state

Salisbury treated the queen much more along Gladstonian than along Disraelian lines, but they were largely at one on major political questions, and certainly so over Ireland. Salisbury defeated the queen over the appointment of Randall Davidson as bishop of Rochester in 1891, but the dispute was a personal one, with the queen wishing to retain Davidson as dean of Windsor, where he played an important role in her spiritual life and in advising on ecclesiastical appointments.

Victoria's aversion to ceremonial continued unabated. It owed much to her dislike of show and to her shyness, while the six attempts to assassinate or assault her during her reign gave substance to her fears about public appearances. Despite the decline of republicanism, she never felt entirely secure in her position, and did not take the allegiance of the poor for granted. Her concern for their welfare—manifested in the later phase of her reign by her support for the Sunday opening of museums, housing reform, and public works schemes for the unemployed—combined feelings of stewardship towards her subjects with a desire to pacify the potentially unruly.

The queen was with difficulty brought to participate in the jubilee celebrations of her coronation. Though there had been some further signs of political and press complaint at her behaviour in 1886, in 1887 the golden jubilee celebrations went off with apparent popular enthusiasm. It was the first of those gatherings of royalties *en masse* which, either for such celebrations or for funerals, were a marked feature of the years before 1914, and it provided a splendid stage on which to display Victoria as the grandmother of Europe. The procession to the service of thanksgiving in Westminster Abbey on 21 June featured royalties from throughout Europe, several Indian princes, the queen of Hawaii, and princes from Japan, Persia, and Siam. The queen's refusal to wear the crown and robes of state—she wore a bonnet laced with diamonds in the simple landau coach—emphasized the public role she chose for herself in her final years: the 'widow of Windsor', her simplicity elevating her above even the majestic trappings of royalty. Though Joseph Chamberlain objected that her visit to Birmingham was insufficiently accompanied by royal paraphernalia, this was a rare complaint. Victoria's self-presentation as a simple, apolitical old lady, remote from wealth and power, was one which the public relished (and contrasted with the flamboyant, etiquette-ridden, politically active monarchies of continental Europe). The jubilee service was followed by a series of tiring events. On 24 June the queen issued a letter of thanks to the nation. The celebrations concluded with army and navy reviews at Aldershot and Spithead respectively, and with a great variety of deputations and presentations. Victoria did not usually on such occasions make speeches, but she often said a few words of thanks, in a clear and audible voice.

When the Unionists lost the general election of 1892, the queen hoped to give public notice of her wish to avoid a fourth Gladstone premiership by sending for Lord Rosebery. Ponsonby dissuaded her from this, and Gladstone formed a government. The queen was careful to make it clear, at least to Ponsonby, that she disliked sending for Gladstone, '(not because she has any personal dislike to him) [but] as she utterly loathes his very dangerous politics' (Ponsonby, 217). In the *Court Circular* she announced that she accepted Salisbury's resignation 'with regret'. Gladstone's last ministry was a miserable episode on both sides, ending with the aged premier unable to extract a promise from his sovereign that she would treat confidentially his plans for retirement. When he did retire, in March 1894, the queen did not ask his advice about a successor. (Constitutional lore is unclear whether she should have done so. When Derby resigned in somewhat analagous circumstances in 1868 Disraeli's succession was already a matter of common agreement; the queen did not directly ask Derby's advice at the time of resignation, though, unlike the more scrupulous Gladstone, he offered it anyway.) The queen sounded out Salisbury about the possibility of another minority Conservative-led government, and then turned to Rosebery (rather than Sir William Harcourt), whom she had long championed among the Liberals. Ignoring a letter from him offering his usual series of objections to taking office, the queen invited Rosebery to form a government, which he agreed to do. Rosebery's skilful letters and his widowed status promised a revival of a Disraelian relationship, but his government soon resigned, in June 1895, following defeat in the Commons.

'Poor dear Queen'

Victoria's diamond jubilee

With Rosebery's defeat Victoria turned happily again to Lord Salisbury, 'who has so faithfully served her before' (*Letters*, 3rd ser., 2.523), and Salisbury's third premiership saw out her reign. This was the nineteenth occasion (ignoring abortive attempts and failed resignations) on which Victoria had played the monarch's role in initiating a new government, and Salisbury was the last of her ten prime ministers. In her late seventies she was inevitably growing tired, although a challenge to British prestige could still draw out one of her inimitable rebukes. When her grandson Kaiser Wilhelm congratulated the president of the Transvaal on foiling the Jameson raid in January 1896 in the so-called Kruger telegram, she fired off a letter regretting his actions, 'as your Grandmother to whom you have always shown so much affection and of whose example you have always spoken with so much respect' (*Letters*, 3rd ser., 3.8); his explanations she found 'lame and illogical' (ibid., 18). The illness and death of Sir Henry Ponsonby in 1895 marked a major change in the queen's household; he was replaced

The greatest sadness of Victoria's later years was the death of her first son-in-law in 1888, a mere ninety-eight days after he had succeeded his father as German emperor. All Albert's hopes for creating a liberal Germany under the guidance of Vicky and Fritz crashed to the ground, and Vicky's son Willie became emperor and set Germany on the path that led eventually to war with his mother's homeland in 1914. For once the queen acknowledged a grief greater than her own when Albert died: 'You are far more sorely tried than me. I had not the agony of seeing another fill the place of my angel husband which I always felt I could not have borne' (*Darling Child*, 72). More grief followed in January 1892, when the prince of Wales's eldest son, Albert Victor, duke of Clarence, died shortly after becoming engaged to Princess May of Teck. Victoria approved unequivocally when Princess May became engaged instead to Clarence's brother George. The death of Prince Henry of Battenberg in 1896 was a still greater blow: chafing somewhat under the restrictions of living under his mother-in-law's roof, Beatrice's husband had persuaded the queen to allow him to serve in the Asante expedition, but he caught a fever and died on a hospital ship. 'My heart aches for my darling child, who is so resigned and submissive', Victoria wrote (*Letters*, 3rd ser., 3.26). The tone of restrained jollity which had come into the royal household with Beatrice's marriage never really returned, although the queen was generally serene and often cheerful. She was surrounded now by a circle of devoted women courtiers whose veneration of the 'poor dear Queen' made her comfortable.

The Indian princes who had attended the jubilee celebrations in 1887 had captured Victoria's imagination, and she was delighted to acquire two Indian servants of her own. The first of many, they attended the queen in Indian dress, adding an exotic touch to the humdrum household. The queen was, for her time and place, remarkably free from racial prejudice:

> she had a very strong feeling (and she has few stronger) that the natives and coloured races should be treated with every kindness and affection, as brothers, not—as alas! Englishmen too often do—as totally different beings to ourselves, fit only to be crushed and shot down. (*Letters*, 2nd ser., 2.361)

One of the original pair of servants, Abdul Karim, soon made it clear that he was no mere domestic: he had been a *munshi*, or clerk, in India, and the queen soon promoted him to teach her Hindustani. The munshi, as he was known, was the last recipient of the queen's passionate devotion to her servants: in her eyes he could do no wrong. The household and her own children, on the other hand, greeted this newly ascendant servant with the horror that had formerly been reserved for John Brown. He became a constant source of friction, with the queen insisting that he be treated as a member of the household rather than as a servant, while the household—who did not on the whole share the queen's liberal views towards people of other races—abominated him. They accused him of spying, of unduly influencing the queen in favour of Muslim rather than Hindu Indians, of feathering his own nest at the queen's expense. Most heinous of all, they found out that his father was not the respectable surgeon he had claimed, but an apothecary at the gaol at Agra: Indians of good birth could be tolerated, but the household felt they were being asked to dine with their servants. Rows over the munshi punctuated the queen's last years. Politics aside, the queen's interests were now those of the very elderly: her family, her health, her memories of the past, and her expectation of reunion with Albert, so long delayed.

On 23 September 1896 the queen noted in her journal that 'To-day is the day on which I have reigned longer, by a day, than any English sovereign' (*Letters*, 3rd ser., 3.79). She rejected suggestions that the event be marked by any public ceremony, asking that they be put off 'until I had completed the sixty years next June'. Victoria had long since stopped expecting to die any moment: at seventy-seven she fully expected still to occupy her throne a year later. The sixtieth anniversary of her accession (20 June 1897) was celebrated in a service of thanksgiving in St George's Chapel, Windsor, with her family around her. The golden jubilee had been celebrated ten years earlier by the royal families of Europe; the queen had deprecated the cost and the difficulties of housing so many of her royal relations at one time, and refused to do so again. The colonial secretary, Joseph Chamberlain, was credited with the idea of turning the jubilee into a celebration of empire: colonial premiers and their wives would not have to be put up in the royal palaces, and their invitation would be a compliment to the colonies they represented.

The public celebration of the diamond jubilee took place on 22 June: the queen was driven in procession in an open carriage through the streets of London to St Paul's

Cathedral, where a brief outdoor service was held. One German princess expressed horror: 'after 60 years Reign, to thank God in the Street!!!' (J. Pope-Hennessy, *Queen Mary*, 1959, 335), but it was a popular and pragmatic solution for Victoria, whose lameness would have made leaving and re-entering her carriage in public an undignified matter. The return journey took the queen over London Bridge and along the Borough Road, allowing many of her poorer subjects the chance of a glimpse of her. They were 'just as enthusiastic and orderly as elsewhere', she remarked (*Letters*, 3rd ser., 3.176). Thus the queen who hated pomp and ceremony inaugurated the practice of large-scale royal ceremonial which defined the twentieth-century monarchy.

The end of an era, 1898–1901

Victoria's powers were fading by 1898. Confined to a wheelchair, her eyesight giving out, her digestion troubled, and her memory occasionally lapsing, she looked set for a gentle decline into senility, a possible regency, and death. She was saved from this ignominy by the worsening of relations between Britain and Germany, by the outbreak of the South African War, and by her own determination. The Kaiser's deep ambivalence towards his British heritage kept him personally respectful towards his grandmother, but his bellicosity worried her deeply: in 1898 she was moved to send a messenger to the leading newspaper editors, asking them to moderate their tone towards Germany, in hopes that it would be reciprocated (in fact, Wilhelm interpreted the milder tone which prevailed for a time as a sign of weakness). She celebrated the victory at Omdurman and the retaking of Khartoum in September: Gordon was avenged at last. Gordon's destroyer, her old enemy Gladstone, had died in May; crippled by her absolute honesty, she could not bring herself to offer a public tribute of regret. She was worried by the Dreyfus affair, and when Dreyfus was convicted afresh in September 1899 sent *en clair* telegrams to Salisbury and her ambassador in France deploring 'this monstrous horrible sentence against this poor martyr Dreyfus' (Weintraub, 603). She was excoriated in the French right-wing press.

Rising tensions in southern Africa occupied Victoria throughout the summer of 1899, and the declaration of war in October gave her a new lease of life. She inspected troops from her wheelchair, visited the sick and injured as they returned to Britain, and at Christmas gave a tin of chocolate to each soldier serving in the field. She corresponded supportively with her army commanders (she never undermined morale in the field by criticizing the often disastrous conduct of the war), but regularly berated her ministers about the inefficiency of the bureaucracy of war and particularly the medical provision for the sick and wounded, which in many ways had not improved since the Crimean War. During 'black week' (10–15 December 1899), when the British suffered a series of devastating reverses, she famously rebuked the downhearted A. J. Balfour with the positively Elizabethan declaration 'Please understand that there is no one depressed in *this* house; we are not interested in the possibilities of defeat; they do not exist' (Weintraub, 611). To mark the seriousness of the situation the queen broke with her previously inflexible routine, and instead of leaving Windsor after the anniversary of Albert's death to spend Christmas at Osborne, she remained at Windsor. She told Marie Mallet, 'After the Prince Consort's death I wished to die, but *now* I wish to live and do what I can for my country and those I love' (*Life with Queen Victoria*, 213).

The reliefs of Kimberley and Ladysmith in February 1900 were cause for celebration, and the queen thanked the City of London (which had raised and financed a regiment for the war) by making an official visit in March. The streets thronged with enthusiastic and loyal subjects: while Victoria reigned, the empire was yet safe. But Britain was deeply unpopular in Europe, not just in Germany, where Wilhelm used the war to fan hatred of his mother's country, but also in France and Italy, and the aged and increasingly enfeebled Victoria was savagely caricatured as an imperial tyrant. The political climate made her annual visit to the French riviera unwise, and instead, inspired by the Irish troops relieving Ladysmith, she went to Ireland. The visit was her own idea: 'I must honestly confess it is *not* entirely to please the Irish, but partly because I expect to enjoy myself', she said (*Life with Queen Victoria*, 192). Security was tight for her three-week stay at Viceregal Lodge in Dublin, and the queen saw only cheerful crowds of well-wishers.

During 1900, as the war in south Africa dragged on, Victoria's health declined rapidly. She had trouble sleeping at night and staying awake during the day. Her appetite, once so enormous, was gone, and she was able to eat only infrequently. And, with the powers of its linchpin fading, the structures of court life began disintegrating as well. But the queen still saw her ministers, still read (or had read aloud to her) the official papers, still fired off her regular hail of letters to her widespread family, politicians, her army officers, and representatives overseas, although now they were usually dictated to her daughters Princess Helena and Princess Beatrice. Victoria's second son, Affie, the duke of Edinburgh and duke of Coburg, died from cancer of the throat on 31 July; Empress Frederick was dying slowly and in excruciating pain from spinal cancer (although she outlived her mother by six months); and on 27 October Victoria's grandson Prince Christian Victor (Christle), son of Princess Helena, died from enteric fever on his way home from south Africa, where he had been serving with the army. This death brought the queen back from Balmoral to Windsor, where she remained for the annual service at Frogmore mausoleum on 14 December before going to Osborne for Christmas. It was an unfestive occasion, despite the presence of children and grandchildren, the gloom deepened by the death—in waiting to the last—of Jane, Lady Churchill, on Christmas day. Lady Churchill was the last of the queen's ladies from Albert's time (Lady Ely had died in 1890, the duchess of Atholl in 1898), and Victoria wept over her passing.

The court circular continued to state that the queen drove out daily, but this was often a polite fiction intended to disguise Victoria's decline. She could no longer write in her journal, but dictated entries to her granddaughter 'Thora' (Princess Helena Victoria); after 13 January 1901 even this stopped, and the record which had begun in 1832 was ended. Her last, characteristic order, on 15 January, was that the ambassador in Berlin should decline an honour offered him by the Kaiser. Joseph Chamberlain was the last minister to have an audience with her, on 11 January, but he tactfully withdrew as it was obviously beyond the queen's strength. On 16 January she did not get up, and she never left her bed again. On 19 January a bulletin about the queen's health was issued for the first time, and her family began gathering at Osborne. On 21 January the prince of Wales arrived, with his brother Arthur, duke of Connaught, and his nephew Kaiser Wilhelm, who had rushed from Berlin on hearing the news. The queen slept, rousing herself to ask for her Pomeranian dog, and to wonder whether the prince of Wales should be told she was ill. Her son was at her side, and she seemed to recognize him; her last audible word was 'Bertie'. After lunch the family again gathered at her bedside, while the vicar of Whippingham, and Randall Davidson, now bishop of Winchester and still the queen's favourite clergyman, prayed aloud. Davidson recited Henry Newman's 'Lead, kindly light'; whether she heard or not, it was a fitting accompaniment:

> So long Thy power hath blest me, sure it still
> Will lead me on,
> O'er moor and fen, o'er crag and torrent, till
> The night is gone.
> And with the morn those Angel voices smile,
> Which I have loved long since, and lost awhile.

At Osborne House, at half past six in the evening of 22 January 1901, in her eighty-second year and the sixty-fourth year of her reign, Victoria died.

Monarchy restored and remembered

Victorian's funeral

Lytton Strachey captured perfectly the sense of dismay which swept the country as news of Victoria's failing health was announced:

> It appeared as if some monstrous reversal of the course of nature was about to take place. The vast majority of her subjects had never known a time when Queen Victoria had not been reigning over them. She had become an indissoluble part of their whole scheme of things, and that they were about to lose her appeared a scarcely possible thought. (*Queen Victoria*, 1921, 309)

Victoria had left detailed instructions about her funeral: her cousin Princess Mary, duchess of Teck, had died in 1897 without leaving a will, and the queen had immediately set her own wishes on paper. Despite her commitment to the forms of personal mourning, the queen hated 'black funerals', and decreed that her own was to be white and gold. She was proud of being a soldier's daughter and the head of the armed forces, and hers was to be a military funeral, her coffin to be pulled on a gun carriage by eight horses. Under no circumstances was her body to be embalmed. In addition to these general commands she had also written a set of instructions 'for my Dressers to be opened directly after my death and to be always taken about and kept by the one who may be travelling with me' (M. Reid, *Ask Sir James*, 1989, 215), which were kept secret from her family, and contained a list of items which were to be placed in her coffin.

There was considerable flurry over the arrangements, as Victoria's household—now superseded by that of the new king—sought to carry out their last duties to the queen. With Victoria lying on her bed in a white gown, surrounded by flowers, covered by her wedding veil, Albert's deathbed portrait hung above her head, her last portraits were taken, by Emile Fuchs, Hubert von Herkomer, and an unknown photographer (possibly Sir James Reid). On 25 January the queen's body was placed inside the first of the three coffins she had ordered (made locally after some confusion with the undertakers, Bantings). Beneath her, her dressers and doctor, Sir James Reid, had arranged Prince Albert's dressing gown and a cloak worked for him by their long-dead second daughter, Princess Alice, a plaster cast of Prince Albert's hand, mementoes of virtually every member of her extended family, her servants, and friends, including an array of shawls and handkerchiefs, framed photographs, lockets, and bracelets, and a sprig of heather from Balmoral. Once the family had left the room, Sir James placed a photograph of John Brown and a lock of his hair in the queen's left hand; among the rings she was wearing was the wedding ring of Brown's mother, which he had given to the queen in 1883. The coffin was sealed in the presence of the male members of the royal family, and was brought downstairs to lie in state in a temporary *chapelle ardente*, which more usually served as the dining-room.

On 1 February the queen's body (now encased in a triple coffin of oak, lead, and more oak, weighing half a ton) was placed on a gun carriage and taken to Cowes, where the royal yacht *Alberta* was waiting. Accompanied by Lady Lytton and the Hon. Harriet Phipps, two of her ladies-in-waiting, the queen's body made its last voyage across the Solent, between two rows of battleships and cruisers, one comprising thirty ships from the British navy, the other vessels sent in tribute from Germany, France, Portugal, and Japan, firing minute guns to mark her passing. The coffin remained overnight on the *Alberta* before proceeding to London on the following day by train. From Victoria Station the cortège moved along streets hung with purple cloth and white satin bows, the lampposts adorned with evergreen wreaths (provided by the activity of a volunteer ladies' committee), and through parks packed sixty deep with silent, black-clad crowds, to Paddington Station, where it joined the royal train to Windsor. At Windsor the coffin was placed once more on a gun carriage, but a horse shied and broke the traces, so the coffin was pulled by a guard of sailors to St George's Chapel, where the short funeral service was held. The coffin remained in the Albert memorial chapel until 4 February, when it was taken to the mausoleum at Frogmore, and, in a ceremony witnessed only by her family, Victoria was laid to rest with Albert. The Marochetti effigy of the queen which had been made at the same time as that of the prince consort had been found (after some difficulty), walled up in a storeroom in Windsor, and was placed over the tomb.

The queen and the later Victorian constitution

To the last the queen remained a very active and fertile element of the working constitution. She had safeguarded her prerogative jealously and zealously, and handed over to her son a monarchy much more engaged in the day-to-day working of the government than was apparent to her subjects. Indeed, given the democratization of politics which occurred during her reign, the royal prerogative was much less altered than might have been expected. It cannot be said that this was the result of the queen's skill, for she had by her partisan behaviour placed the monarchy in considerable danger, to the extent that she had been warned by William Gladstone about the serious long-term dangers to the monarchy of the partisan unionism of the court:

> At the present juncture, the views of Your Majesty's actual advisers, although now supported by a majority of the people (to say nothing of the people of the Colonies, and the English-speaking race at large), are hardly at all represented, and as Mr Gladstone believes, are imperfectly known, in the powerful social circles with which Your Majesty has ordinary personal intercourse. (*Letters*, 3rd ser., 2.172)

Through the loyalty and reticence of political leaders on both sides this issue was largely kept out of public discussion, and the Liberals brought forward no plan for the reform of the monarchy during the queen's reign. The concentration of radical critics on royal finances in the early 1870s produced only superficial discussion, for the issue was not really the financing of the monarchy but the role of the royal family in national life. Partisanship on the part of the monarch was, of course, nothing new; what was new was that the monarch could no longer give effect to partisan views. However much the queen might loathe Liberal governments led by Gladstone, even she did not think that she had the power to prevent them. The removal, before the start of her reign, of crown electoral control through rotten boroughs, and the consolidation of the political parties after the uncertainties of the mid-century, meant that the role of the monarch in making ministries was at best confined, except in very unusual circumstances, to a choice of personalities, and even then, as the queen found in 1880 and on other occasions, the political process rather than her will was ultimately decisive.

In the second half of her reign, it was only in 1895— the choice of Rosebery—that the queen's will was decisive, and even then only because the Liberals did not object, preferring Rosebery to W. V. Harcourt. In her later years the queen's partisan behaviour was in fact unnecessary, for the objectives of unionism, at least in the short term, were achieved by Lord Salisbury and Joseph Chamberlain; the queen's violent anti-Liberalism in fact could only endanger rather than aid their objectives. The queen was fortunate also in the forbearance of her successor, who handled his mother tactfully; the prince of Wales did not press himself forward, even when, at fifty-one, he experienced the humiliation of the queen's refusing Gladstone's suggestion that he should regularly see copies of the cabinet papers that were sent to the monarch.

For her part, Queen Victoria's sense of duty and pertinacity did much to maintain the monarchy in the working constitution. Her willingness to read every paper put before her, her speed in spotting when a paper which should have been sent to her had been withheld, her tenacity with respect to appointments, whether ecclesiastical, military, political, or diplomatic, and her long experience and encyclopaedic knowledge of European dynastic politics meant that she retained the respect of her premiers, most of whom were of high intellectual calibre, even when they differed from her. Disraeli's treatment of the queen as his 'Faery' creates a highly misleading view of this tough-minded, resourceful woman who, though she disliked political life, learned the tricks of its trade and knew how to anticipate the manoeuvres of its practitioners. The queen was very rarely taken by surprise by any political development, though her correspondence is often larded with such words as 'alarm' and 'shock', and those who dealt with her knew they had little chance of getting round her by sleight of hand. One result of this was that she often called forth from ministers memoranda on policy matters which were their most cogent statements of the case.

Victoria acted boldly in the pursuit of her own objectives, and was never embarrassed. Her appointment of Liberal secretaries, Grey and Ponsonby, was a sensible arrangement for dealing with the party with which she was most likely to be in dispute, but it placed an extra weight on her, for it meant that she had to formulate her views without much reference to her secretary, the person with whom, after the death of Albert, confidential political discussion most naturally occurred. The queen, in effect, relied on Ponsonby to allow her to form a view and then to see that her view was presented in as acceptable a form as possible to her ministers; Ponsonby became adept at delaying letters and suggesting alternative, less combative ways of expressing points. The queen, while feeling that she should express her views as if she was directly responsible for policy, also realized the impracticability of that position and relied on Ponsonby to reconcile the two; this he was stoically successful in doing. The queen did not see herself as partisan, since her view of politics, like that of many Conservatives, defined the national interest in terms of her own views. For her, unionism was self-evidently right.

Victoria was not a willing agent in the development of the modern British constitutional monarchy; but it began to form itself around her during her reign even so. The prerogatives she left to a monarch who was willing to be active publicly as well as privately were, however, considerable, as her son's forays into foreign policy were soon to show. In 1837 Victoria had inherited a tarnished crown, its powers waning, its popularity sinking. She left it to her son in 1901 restored and renewed, but fundamentally altered. Victoria had felt it her duty to engage actively with ministers in the business of government; her successors enjoyed less in the way of political authority. Ironically, it was as ceremonial figureheads and model families that Britain's monarchs reigned in the twentieth century. Victoria had been the last Hanoverian.

Victoria's reputation

There can be few lives more monumentally documented than that of Queen Victoria. It was a process she began herself, for the habit of journal-keeping was instilled in her at an early age. She left her journal to her daughter Beatrice in her will, and the princess religiously transcribed those portions she thought fit for posterity and destroyed the originals, but even the bowdlerized journal is an invaluable source for historians. She was a prolific writer of letters, personal and political, vast numbers of which have survived. Her official life brought her into contact with politicians, diplomatists, soldiers, churchmen, foreign royalties, visiting dignitaries, artists, writers, musicians, actors, scientists—anybody with any pretensions to importance in Victorian Britain crossed her path at some time or other. She was, moreover, an object of great curiosity to virtually everybody who met her, many of whom recorded their impressions and experiences. Even restricting the search to printed sources, it is possible to find Victoria's views on a huge range of subjects and her impressions of the people she met. She was also one of the most painted, sculpted, drawn, caricatured, and photographed people of her day: from the watercolour sketch made by Paul Fischer in 1819 to the photograph taken on her deathbed there were few incidents and relationships in her life which were not captured in visual form.

Biographies of the queen began appearing early in her reign. Among the first was Agnes Strickland's *Queen Victoria from her Birth to her Bridal* (1840), which the queen informed the author was wildly inaccurate; the volume was withdrawn. At the time of her jubilees many accounts of her life appeared, often in the form of salutary and improving tales for children; her son-in-law the marquess of Lorne produced one of the earliest commemorative volumes after her death, *V. R. I.: Her Life and Empire* (1901). The timing of the queen's

death was inconvenient for the editors of the *Dictionary of*
National Biography: the intended end date had been 1900.
An additional volume was hastily added, the 93,000 words
on the late queen being written by the second editor, Sidney
Lee, and subsequently published separately.

Lee's *Queen Victoria* was the first full biography to appear,
and the only one not to benefit from the publication of the
Letters of Queen Victoria, the first series of which appeared
in 1907, edited by Lord Esher and A. C. Benson; it covered
the queen's life from her birth until the death of the prince
consort. (In 1912 Esher edited the two-volume *Girlhood of
Queen Victoria*, which contained valuable extracts from her
early, uncut journal.) The *Letters of Queen Victoria* (two
subsequent series were published in 1926–8 and 1930–32,
edited by G. E. Buckle) provides the basis for every student
of Victoria to whom the Royal Archives are inaccessible.
While the letters do not present a 'warts and all' image of the
queen, they are surprisingly frank in their portrayal of the
queen's political role and private opinions: as Frank Hardie
pointed out in *The Political Influence of Queen Victoria,
1861–1901* (1935), the queen had so successfully projected
the public image of a charming old lady, benignly and
impartially presiding over the welfare of her nation, that
readers were surprised, even shocked, to discover how far she
had taken an active—and sometimes obstructive—role in
political affairs. The Gladstone family were so distressed by
the *Letters* that they arranged to publish the correspondence
between the queen and Gladstone; this showed rather more
clearly both the prime minister's side of the story and how
far the queen used her position to hinder his ministries.

Lytton Strachey's biography (1921) disappoints readers expecting a Bloomsbury attack: his Victoria is rather sympathetically portrayed in her 'vitality, conscientiousness, pride, and simplicity' (Strachey, *Queen Victoria*, 1921, 306). Of the modern biographies of Victoria, Lady Longford's (1964) remains indispensable: based on a close reading of the extensive archival sources, including Princess Beatrice's transcript of the journal, her *Victoria R. I.* is a rounded life, which perceptively integrates the political with the personal.

Few people are truly legends in their own lifetimes: Victoria was one such, and her mythic status increased with the passage of time. Her image continues to surround us: few towns in Britain are without a statue of Victoria, a Victoria park, hospital, theatre, hall, or museum, or a street named for her. Despite the disintegration of the British empire, statues of Victoria remain in place in former colonies from India to the Bahamas, New Zealand to Canada, South Africa to Singapore. The most conspicuously removed statue of the queen was that which stood in Dublin; dismantled after independence, it was eventually given to the people of Australia and stands in Sydney.

The ubiquity of the stern, matriarchal Victoria in public sculpture ingrained the image of the queen as an unsmiling prude on the general consciousness. Victoria felt it undignified and unqueenly to be painted or photographed smiling: a rare photograph of her smile captured by Charles Knight in 1898 reveals the transformation. The chilling put-down 'We are not amused' is perhaps the best-known 'fact' about the queen, although its provenance is unclear. Victoria's determination to present a regal face to posterity thus did her a

great disservice, for a readiness to be pleased, and indeed
amused, was one of her more endearing characteristics. She
had a tendency towards the lachrymose, but there were
many genuine causes for grief in her life. Nor was she a
prude, as the published letters to her daughter Empress
Frederick reveal, but she did have a great sense of modesty:
even at eighty she held her fan in front of her face when
speaking of a *risqué* play to a man—'delightfully young,
modest and naive!' commented an observer (*Life with Queen
Victoria*, 170). She could be rude, dictatorial, selfish (especially in old age); she was also shy, honest, and humble in
the face of virtue in others and in the sight of the God who
she fervently believed watched over her and her country.

After the First World War, and Lytton Strachey's assaults on
the preceding generation, ' Victorian' came to mean hypo-
critical, mealy-mouthed, prudish; the adjectives multiplied,
and attached themselves to Victoria's own reputation, in
defiance of the evidence. For a long time the Victorians were
widely misunderstood: their closeness in time made it difficult to comprehend just how different they were from their
successors. Earnestness can easily look like cant to an unsym-
pathetic audience; moral certitude looks like hypocrisy when
failure to meet high standards rather than the attempt to do
so is taken as the measure. In her sincerity, her enthusiasms,
her effort to do her duty, Victoria was truly Victorian: the age
rightly bears her name.

Sources

Victoria's letters and writings

The letters of Queen Victoria, ed. A. C. Benson, Lord Esher [R. B. Brett], and G. E. Buckle, 9 vols. (1907–32) · *The girlhood of Queen Victoria: a selection from her majesty's diaries between the years 1832 and 1840*, ed. Viscount Esher [R. B. Brett], 2 vols. (1912) · *Dearest child: letters between Queen Victoria and the princess royal, 1858–1861*, ed. R. Fulford (1964) · *Dearest mama: letters between Queen Victoria and the crown princess of Prussia, 1861–1864*, ed. R. Fulford (1968) · *Your dear letter: private correspondence of Queen Victoria and the crown princess of Prussia, 1865–1871*, ed. R. Fulford (1971) · *Darling child: private correspondence of Queen Victoria and the crown princess of Prussia, 1871–1878*, ed. R. Fulford (1976) · *Beloved mama: letters between Queen Victoria and the German crown princess, 1878–1885*, ed. R. Fulford (1976) · *Beloved and darling child: last letters between Queen Victoria and her eldest daughter, 1886–1901*, ed. A. Ramm (1990) · Queen Victoria, *Leaves from the journal of our life in the highlands*, ed. A. Helps (1868) · Queen Victoria, *More leaves from the journal of a life in the highlands, from 1862 to 1882* (1884) · T. Martin, *The life of ... the prince consort*, 5 vols. (1875–80) · B. Connell, ed., *Regina v Palmerston* (1962) · P. Guedalla, ed., *The queen and Mr Gladstone*, 2 vols. (1933)

Biographies

E. Longford, *Victoria RI* (1964) · S. Weintraub, *Victoria: biography of a queen* (1988) · M. Charlot, *Victoria: the young queen* (1991) ·

C. Woodham-Smith, *Queen Victoria: her life and times*, 1: *1819–1861* (1972) · W. Arnstein, *Queen Victoria* (2003) · L. Strachey, *Queen Victoria* (1921)

Studies

L. Vallone, *Becoming Victoria* (2001) · M. Warner, *Queen Victoria's sketchbook* (1979–81) · K. Hudson, *A royal conflict* (1994) · D. Thompson, *Queen Victoria: gender and power* (1990) · G. Rowell, *Queen Victoria goes to the theatre* (1978) · F. Prochaska, *Royal bounty: the making of a welfare monarchy* (1995) · F. Hardie, *The political influence of Queen Victoria* (1935) · W. Kuhn, *Democratic royalism* (1996) · R. Williams, *The contentious crown* (1997) · A. Munich, *Queen Victoria's secrets* (1996) · A. Ponsonby, *Sir Henry Ponsonby: his life from his letters* (1942) · *Life with Queen Victoria: Marie Mallet's letters from court, 1887–1901*, ed. V. Mallet (1968) · Mrs S. Erskine, *Twenty years at court* (1916) · H. C. G. Matthew, *Gladstone*, 2 vols. (1986–95) · R. Blake, *Disraeli* (1966) · W. F. Monypenny and G. E. Buckle, *The life of Benjamin Disraeli*, 6 vols. (1910–20) · M. Reid, *Ask Sir James* (1989) · T. Aronson, *Grandmama of Europe: the crowned descendants of Queen Victoria* (1973) · L. Mitchell, *Lord Melbourne* (1997) · R. Lamont-Brown, *John Brown: Queen Victoria's highland servant* (2000) · A. L. Kennedy, *My dear duchess* (1956)

Index